HIRAM HILL HOMESTEAD
Back to the Land at 50

HIRAM HILL HOMESTEAD
Back to the Land at 50

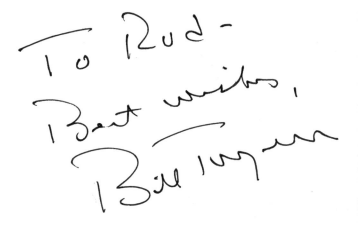

To Rud –
Best wishes,
Bill Turgeon

Bill Turgeon

Mill City Press
Minneapolis, MN

Mill City Press, Inc.
212 3rd Avenue North, Suite 570
Minneapolis, MN 55401
612-455-2293
www.millcitypress.net

ISBN - 1-934937-02-9
ISBN - 978-0-934937-02-0
LCCN - 2008926095

Cover Design by Brent Meyers
Typeset by Sophie Chi

Printed in the United States of America

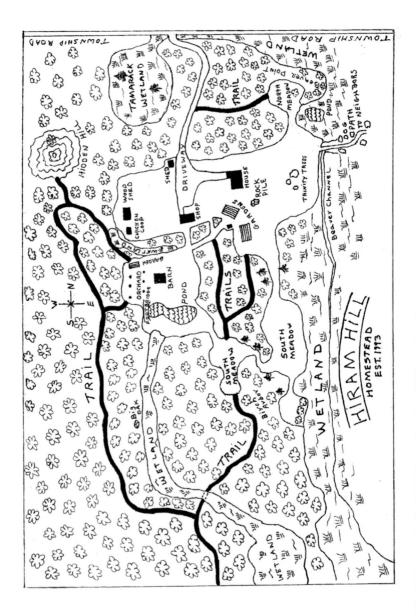

CONTENTS

ACKNOWLEDGMENTS

I am grateful to my sister-in-law, Jennifer Schartz,
for reading the manuscript twice and for making
many helpful suggestions along the way.
Her sharp editing skills improved my copy significantly.

This book would not have materialized without
the support given to me by my wife, Kathy.
She encouraged me to tell our story,
and I appreciate all she does for me.

KATHY'S PAINTINGS

My wife, Kathy, would have made an ideal Kansas homesteader in the 1800s. Frugal and hardworking, she would have stood firmly at her husband's side to face the hardships that inevitably came with frontier life. Some farmers and their wives gave up after living through too many hard times. But other homesteaders stayed put despite their trials, thanks in large part to the determination of strong frontier women. They were a source of unwavering support and encouragement to their families.

I know Kathy would have made a good frontier wife because she was my source of encouragement in our own little "pioneering" effort in the 1990s. And like the husbands of the early settlers, my determination to build a place where there was no place before might have disappeared in the wind without her steady hand. She's a natural when it comes to making the best of what life gives you because she approaches each day with innate gratitude for what she has and what seems possible.

It was just that sort of attitude that led her to enroll in a community college painting class in 1975 which, unbeknownst to her, would have a meaningful connection many years later to a new and rewarding life on the land with a husband she had not yet met. Practical and open to a new challenge, she took her very first painting class because she wanted to have an original painting to hang in her mobile home in Kansas. "Original paintings are expensive," she reasoned, "and I can't afford to buy one right now, so I will take the class and paint one myself." Actually, she finished not one, but two, acrylic pictures that amazingly foreshadowed what her life was to become years later. She started a third that, like the first two, also told something of what was to come. Only a few years earlier she had returned to her Kansas hometown to rebuild her life after a disappointing marriage and a divorce. She found a teaching job in a local public elementary school, bought the trailer house from her brother, and reconnected with life in her home community. An art class at the college seemed like a good thing to do.

With orange, rust, gold, and browns from her palette, she painted the first picture by copying in her own hand an original oil painting by an unknown artist that hung in her grandmother Patti Ma's home in Kansas. Kathy's painting shows a rural autumn scene under a pale blue, partly cloudy sky. A slightly curving gravel track runs past a tall oak tree and toward a small house and a grove of trees in full autumn colors. Meadows with brown grass, bushes, and fallen leaves, lay on both sides of the road, and a row of old, leaning cedar fence posts suggests a one-time livestock pasture. A closer look reveals that the house sits on a small hill since the land seems to drop off behind it, beckoning the viewer to step into this world and discover the joys of woods and meadows on a golden fall day. You could find this landscape throughout rural New England. But it can be found wherever there are oak trees, hills, ponds, and fields. Though the painting depicts the commonplace, to me it is the most beautiful tableau in the world, and, as these pages will soon attest, it has played a significant role in my life and my spouse's. Kathy's canvas, about half the size of the original oil painting in her grandmother's house, first graced the living room of her trailer home, and, later, it was on display in a house she bought in her hometown. Then, following our marriage in 1981, it has occupied a prominent place in the several homes where we have lived. And it was on the walls in those homes that the beauty and meaning of this picture over time helped me clarify the vague discontent I struggled with in my life. Years earlier, a promising newspaper career came to an abrupt end with a draft notice, followed by four years of military service and time in Vietnam, with a wife and two babies left behind. This turn of events seemed to rob me of some of my youthful assurance. Yet, nothing did that like the divorce that followed a few years later. Only after my marriage to Kathy did I seem to recapture my youthful purpose, although a vague sense of dissatisfaction remained within me as I dutifully attended to the needs and demands of home, work, church, and community.

On countless evenings following supper, when Kathy and I would sit in our living room with a cup of coffee to discuss the day's events or perhaps just listen to some music, I would look at her painting. I studied it in detail and imagined what might lay beyond the house, across the meadow and down the hill. I loved the colors and the glow of autumn that she had captured with her brush, and I wanted to step into this scene and walk the land, stopping and turning to take in the panorama. Fall is my favorite season, so I suppose that is why the picture occupied such a powerful place in my psyche. But even more than that, it seemed to evoke a feeling of what I thought life should be or what I hoped it might be – or perhaps what I had once known growing up on a farm. Such a strong response from within probably betrayed a hidden sadness that seemed to take hold in me at times, no doubt related to the disappointments of the past, the loss of my father when I was 22, and the difficulties trying to raise children hurt by divorce. But not until later did I see any connection between what the picture seemed to say to me and how such a place could help me overcome my own doubts. At the time it was enough to wish that I could walk down that little road in the painting and feel the sun's warm October rays on my shoulders. Kathy had painted something that gladdened my heart, but certainly there was no reason to think it foretold something more, let alone a country place of our own where we could stand on a hillside ablaze in color and enjoy the sunshine.

Kathy completed a second painting during the art class that today hangs in her parents' home in Kansas. The landscape, inspired by a picture she found in a magazine, depicts another rural fall scene, with lots of orange, brown, and gold colors. This time, Kathy painted a barn and a house situated up on a slope, with lots of turning trees giving color and warmth to the scene. She had no idea that her two pictures contained nearly all of the elements she would much later see on a piece of property she and her future husband would one day occupy in northern Minnesota. But there was something more.

She started, but did not finish, a third painting showing high, billowing storm clouds on the horizon. She called the picture, "There's Got to Be a Morning After," the name taken from Maureen McGovern's hit song, *The Morning After*. Kathy never finished painting the picture because it was supposed to be an original conception, and she couldn't decide what to depict below the storm clouds. That would come later in real terms after we found a piece of land and built a homestead. From my point of view, the unfinished and unframed painting, which still sits on a shelf in our basement storage room today, simply points to the future and asks viewers to fill in the blank space with their own hopes and dreams. It was not before passing through a terrible summer storm on the very day that the two of us embarked on our homesteading adventure that we could eventually come to understand what these pictures had been telling us for so many years: The land will help you discover your true selves — let go and live!

1

CHOOSING A NEW PATH

July 1, 1997, will be a day Kathy and I always remember, for it marked the ending of our pleasant life in southwestern Minnesota, and the beginning of our new, full-time homesteading adventure 220 miles north amid the woods and lakes of the North Star state. We didn't know what to expect, nor did we have a clear picture of how everything was supposed to work – especially the finances. After all, we gave up two good jobs that paid well and provided benefits to embrace a much less lucrative and highly uncertain life in the country – a life we undoubtedly had romanticized. We had read numerous books by people who undertook similar homesteading ventures and tried to learn from them as much as we could. One of our favorites was *The "Have-More" Plan* (Storey Books) by Ed and Carolyn Robinson, a how-to manual that shows how families with a little land can enjoy "a lot of living." We subscribed to *Mother Earth News, Countryside, Country Journal* and other magazines and read them from cover to cover, learning about the concept of modern-day homesteading and benefiting from the many articles that provide detailed information on how to build wood sheds, raise pigs, grow fruit trees, manage a woodlot, sharpen an ax, and countless other subjects.

Homesteading means different things to different people, but it has come to mean a return to the land for most; a conscious effort to adopt a different, usually simpler, lifestyle than what people normally experience in today's fast-paced America. Just Google "homesteading" on your computer, and you will find thousands of entries dealing with the "back to the land" meaning of the term. For some, homesteading means becoming self-sufficient and energy independent, producing your own food as much as possible and even moving off the electric power grid by using solar power or wind power in its place. Others seek to adopt a rustic lifestyle, living without electricity and shunning most modern conveniences, equipment, and machinery – using a scythe to cut grass for hay or farming with horses, for example. Still others try to adopt a simple lifestyle even while living in the city. Jerry (Jd) Belanger, founder of *Country-side* ("The Magazine of Modern Homesteading"), says it best:

> It's not a single idea, but many ideas and attitudes, including a reverence for nature and a preference for country life; a desire for maximum personal self-reliance and creative leisure; a concern for family nurture and community cohesion; a belief that the primary reward of work should be well-being rather than money; a certain nostalgia for the supposed simplicities of the past and an anxiety about the technological and bureaucratic complexities of the present and the future; and a taste for the plain and functional.

Kathy and I wanted to adopt a simpler lifestyle and learn to do things we had never done before. We wanted to get closer to nature, and we wanted to garden, cut wood, produce some of our own food, raise a few chickens and pigs, and build things we needed with our own hands. We weren't purists and weren't on any mission, but we knew that modern-day homesteading appealed to us and perhaps would help us get in touch with our true selves. We were in our 50s and felt the need for a stimulating change in our lives while we were still able and healthy. And we had some savings in the bank that would make a new and different lifestyle like this a little less worrisome. We had no children of our own, but my two children had finished college and started careers, so I imagine the empty-nest syndrome affected our thinking when we began to look for land.

So, we headed north with a fair amount of preparation and knowledge, but we didn't really know whether it would work out or whether we would soon have to give it up and return to regular jobs and regular pay. When we look back now, we sometimes wonder whether we were thinking straight at the time. I was 55 years old and took early retirement from my job at a state college, thereby assuring a much smaller retirement check and losing our health insurance. Kathy, at 50, gave up her teaching job in a nearby town and headed north thinking that nobody would hire a teacher at her age, and that substitute teaching was probably her best hope for income. She was too young to start receiving a teacher's pension. On top of that, of course, we were giving up our home and comfortable life in a town where we had lots of friends and good neighbors.

We told ourselves from the outset that the best way to assure success was *to stay out of debt*. If we moved north with debt on our shoulders, we would greatly increase our chances of failure and undoubtedly add unneeded stress and concern in our lives. Both of us have always been frugal, buying for the most part only what we need and having the fortitude to say no when desire seems ready to overtake good sense. We didn't develop fiscal discipline through hard effort. It's just the way we were brought up. When it comes to spending, we both can apply the brakes without much agonizing. Kathy doesn't carry a credit card and rarely has much cash in her purse. She says that since she is a teacher, there is no sense in having money in her purse to tempt a youngster in her classroom. I spend a lot more than she does on things that aren't necessary, but together we seem to listen to the same drumbeat when it comes to managing money and staying out of debt. No one has ever heard us argue about money, even our dogs.

Thus, we were on the same page when it came to finances. If we were going to undertake this new lifestyle and live on less, we knew this much: We must be debt-free before we move ahead, and we would need to learn to live on less. It would be our chance to see whether there is anything to the adage, *less is more*. Homesteaders have no generally held creed or set of principles to live by, but the notion that less is more fits squarely with the desire to live simply, make do, and do for yourself. Nowhere have we seen that life is any less beautiful or, for that matter, less comfortable, by having more than what is needed. What we have learned is that life generally is more invigorating when you have a greater role in providing for your own well-being. Gardening, splitting firewood, sewing, raising animals, putting up food, making compost, and countless other homestead chores are drudgeries to some, but rewarding enterprises to others. Modern life has much to offer us, and technology is transforming the way we live in breathtaking ways. Homesteaders today rely on computers, cell phones, and other technologies as much as everyone else, but they also possess a strong desire to stay in touch with simpler ways and know the joy that comes by getting their hands dirty in useful and creative tasks. We can buy most anything we need and hire any service we desire as long as we have the money to pay the costs. Conversely, we also can "buy" peace of mind, tranquility, and satisfaction by doing more with less and learning to do things for ourselves – knowing the cost will be our time and effort.

So when Kathy and I began to examine the idea of

modern homesteading and realized that many couples, especially younger ones, were embracing it as well and making life-changing decisions, we knew we were on to something. And so, there we were, on July 1, 1997, ready to take the big step of leaving our reasonably secure life and starting our homesteading journey. The college gave me a nice retirement party that afternoon, and when it was over, we rushed to the real estate office for our four o'clock closing on our home. Earlier, we had removed the last boxes from the house and loaded them into the pickup. We hurriedly swept the floors to make ready for a walk-through with the prospective owner. By five o'clock, we had said our last goodbyes, signed the closing papers, and took possession of an $80,000 check from the sale of the house – the sum we needed to pay for the ongoing construction of our new house up north. We were tired to the bone, but ready to go – happy that everything had gone so well and people were so nice. With the pickup truck loaded with the last of our belongings, and our mini-dachshund, Kirby, perched on Kathy's lap as always, we said a fond goodbye to the town where we had lived for 16 years. We headed north on the state highway as we had done scores of times before – but this time there was no return trip planned

highway. We soon discovered that the storm, with its terrifying straight-line winds and heavy rainfall, caused considerable damage throughout the area. Trees and power lines were knocked down, and there was flooding in low-lying areas.

I couldn't help but think of Kathy's unfinished painting with the storm clouds on the horizon. "Not exactly an auspicious start to our new life," I thought. "I wonder what's next?"

We didn't have to wait very long to find out. The rest of the trip was uneventful, but just days after arriving at our new place, Kirby, our beloved little dog of nine years, became ill and died within hours. We had been busy all day doing finishing work in our house while he stayed in our detached shop, which we were using as a makeshift cabin. We found him in an almost unconscious state when we returned late that afternoon. Kirby had been our constant companion through the years as we searched for property in various parts of the state and then later after we had purchased our land and began to make it our retreat. Kirby, Kathy, and I had made nearly a hundred 440-mile round trips from our home in southwestern Minnesota to our north woods property over a four-year period. His death happened so fast, and there was really nothing we could do. He rode on Kathy's lap to the veterinary clinic, and there on a table, we watched him slip away. We put him in a box, went home, and after a fitful sleep, got up early the next morning and buried him on our hillside beneath an outstretched limb of a big bur oak. Our neighbors across the beaver pond said later they saw us digging on the hillside in the early light and wondered what we were doing.

Both of us were heartbroken and bone-weary after the experience, and although not much was said, I couldn't help wonder whether this was just another sign that we really hadn't thought things through. Maybe I had been foolish to quit my job and pretty much just hope for the best up there in the woods. There was so much to do. The house was unfinished, and we were committed to doing much of the finishing work ourselves. I planned to build the kitchen cabinets, and we were waiting for the mason to construct our masonry heater so we could have heat in the winter. Kathy had been given some little pigs, and they needed a shelter built so we could get them out of the woodshed. Although I wanted pigs eventually, I just didn't want them now when there were so many other things to do. We missed our friends, and really didn't know many people in the area. Progress had been slow, and everything seemed to take so much time. Neither of us had jobs, and the prospects for adding to our limited income were uncertain. Short on sleep, I felt weary and a little discouraged.

Fortunately, Kathy kept a better perspective, reminding me that I don't think all that clearly when I lack sleep. We mourned the loss of our pet, but that was no reason to question our decisions or doubt the choices we had made. She went about her business with a sad heart that day, but made us a good dinner that night, and we started talking about the tasks ahead. By bedtime, we had recounted the many wonderful things that this land had already given us: How we enjoyed our times together building a wood shed, planting trees, putting up firewood, listening to loon and blackbird and snipe, and watching the moon rise in the east over the pond and fields. Our disappointments were minor, and our troubles few.

As things turned out, we made good progress on the house, and soon realized that we should be able to move in by mid-September. Dick, the mason, whistled while he laid up bricks for our masonry heater, and we marveled at his workmanship and care. The neighbor kids came over to visit, and their parents were always ready to help if needed. Moreover, our pigs were doing well in their new shelter and pen. And because of them, I stumbled upon good fortune at the feed store where I bought my pig meal. The owners had two mini-dachshunds, Mickey and Minnie, and the pair had recently produced three pups, one a male with brown fur like Kirby's. The puppy was for sale if I wanted him.

With the feed bags in the back of the GMC, it was a happy drive home that day, and I couldn't wait to tell Kathy that I had found her a new dog – a little brown dachshund that we would name Cooper. As it had turned out, Kirby saw us through the many years of preparation for our move north, but Cooper would see us through the adventurous days ahead as we tried to live out our homesteading dream. Yes, we had made the right decision.

2

LOOKING FOR LAND

When I first saw the land, I knew the search was over. It had all the features we sought: Hills, woods, meadows, ponds and privacy. If I had seen the property when we first started looking, I don't know how I would have reacted, for the truth is, we didn't have a clear idea of what we wanted when we began the four-year quest for something we could call "our place." We were naïve at first – so uncertain and tentative. We wanted to jump, but it was unlikely we would jump quickly. Those days we could talk ourselves out of almost anything. And money was always a factor, of course. College costs had sapped much of our savings in the mid- to late-1980s, so we figured we could put down maybe $5,000 to $10,000 for some property, but not much more. We had to be certain. We had to know that our money would get us what we wanted – if we just could figure out what we wanted.

Our search began in 1989, and it wasn't until 1993 that we found the land we would later call home. At first, we followed a plan concocted over coffee: *Let's find a getaway somewhere, maybe a cabin on a lake or in the woods. Somewhere we could escape to on weekends.* Lots of people do that. Going north in Minnesota on the weekend is like going to the seashore in North Carolina or the mountains in Colorado. It's where you want to be. But we never considered buying lakeshore property seriously because it's expensive, and taxes are high.

Then, early in the search, I took Kathy to the farmstead in northwestern Minnesota where I spent much of my youth. My parents purchased the place in the 1940s and built a home there in 1957, a house constructed with salvaged railroad stockyard lumber and redwood that once served as staves in water tanks for railroad steam engines. The house sat in the middle of a grove of poplars, and the farmstead also featured a garage, pole barn and Quonset-type building. The 17-acre site sat empty at the time, but it was part of a 440-acre farm that was managed by a company in Iowa. I showed Kathy the house, which had been vandalized. The roof leaked, windows were broken, and holes had been punched in the walls. We walked around the over-grown yard, and I showed her what was left of the small plum and cherry orchard my parents had planted. It was fall, and the aspen trees, all painted in gold, stood brilliantly against the blue sky, their leaves trembling in the tender breeze. In spite of the neglect we saw, we both were taken by the beauty of the moment, and it was Kathy who said, "Bill, this would be wonderful. Do you think they would sell it? I just love this place. We could be close to your family and cousins."

Her words stunned me. I never would have guessed that the property would appeal to her, and I needed to find out who owned it now, and whether they would sell. "Rebuilding the old home place – how wonderful would that be?" I thought. Suddenly, we both knew what we wanted – a place in the country where we could focus our energies, making it better, building a future. That's what we needed – something to break us out of the monotony of our safe, secure lives. I was amazed and excited. What a great day!

Alas, our excitement lasted only a couple of weeks because the reply to my letter of inquiry about the farmstead crushed us. They would sell. But the price? $49,000! The Iowa farm management company knew my family connection to the property, but that obviously didn't help. The price was totally unjustified in our view because the Quonset and garage were beyond repair, and the house would require many thousands of dollars to rehabilitate. We were deeply disappointed, of course. Years later, we learned that all the trees and buildings had been razed.

The old homestead would have been a great place to make new again. My memories of happy times there are many, and I once recounted them in a talk before a group of North Dakota Farmers Union county officers. At the time – 1975 – I was going through my divorce and had made an ill-advised decision to leave my job with the Farmers Union for something else. My personal world was falling apart, and I couldn't make much sense of anything. I just wanted to run away. Recalling the past and the happy times I once knew as a youth in front of a crowd of people probably helped disguise the pain I felt over what was going on in my life:

> I remember those times in November, when I walked to the edge of the farmstead in the evening to watch the sun go down, when the sky was gray and the clouds were heavy and streaked with orange, when the trees were bare and leafless, and a cold

wind carried the promise of colder days ahead.

Those are the things you remember when you grow up on a farm.

I remember going out those fall evenings with my dad, out to the beaver dam and creek. We used to trap muskrat and mink, but mostly we would just sit and talk. Dad would tell me where the creek used to run and maybe where he once shot a rabbit.

Those are the things you remember when you grow up on a farm.

I remember, too, in the fall when we harvested our potatoes. My brother and I would go out at day's end to pick up the sacks of potatoes the workers had filled during the day. We piled the sacks on the flatbed as high as we could, and then my brother would drive the tractor back home with me riding atop the sacks. I could smell the dirt and potatoes and the new gunny sacks, and it was just me and the darkening sky.

Those are the things you remember when you grow up on a farm.

I remember those hot days in July and August when we were harvesting wheat or oats or barley, and my mother and sister would drive out with lunch at four o'clock. We would stop the combine and the truck and sit in the shade of those machines to eat our sandwiches.

Those are the things you remember when you grow up on a farm.

I also remember the many evenings when I went out to the gravel road running past our farm with my baseball bat. I would bat rocks from the road, sometimes imagining myself in Fenway Park in Boston or Comiskey Park in Chicago. Occasionally, I would really connect with one – and I knew it was a home run. But mostly, I would settle for pop-ups, singles, and strike-outs.

And I also remember those January nights on the farm, when the temperature would drop to 40 below. I'd walk outside to that same road at 10 or 11 just to experience the total silence of the moment, broken only by the crunch of my footsteps in the snow or the sound of a poplar tree cracking from the extreme cold.

Those are the things you remember as you grow up on a farm.

After realizing my family's old place would not be ours, we sort of gave up on our search for a time, but picked it up again in the spring. This is the way it would go: We would search, find properties that interested us, and then learn that they weren't for sale. Even time with real estate agents proved fruitless. But, by now we had a clear idea of what we were searching for. And even if we stopped looking for a while, the passion would rekindle, and off we would go again on some wild goose chase.

There were lots of places to look. We spent many hours driving through Becker, Douglas, Ottertail, and Todd counties in central Minnesota, areas with rolling hills, ponds, lakes, maples, and oaks. We also roamed the Trail Hills not far from my hometown in northwestern Minnesota and liked the idea of retiring there and being close to family and relatives, as we had hoped earlier. Most of the time, we just drove through the country-side not knowing what land was for sale or even if any land were on the market. More than once, we would find a place that interested us, perhaps with an empty farmstead or abandoned buildings, and then try to find out the names of the owners. I wrote letters to several people out of state, relatives who had acquired land that sat empty, but always it was to no avail: The land wasn't for sale. In the Trail Hills area we discovered a beautiful farmstead surrounded by several ponds with lots of trees and some small fields adjoining it. No one was living there, and the place really got our blood pumping. I tracked down the name of the owner, who turned out to be a woman in Oregon, the daughter of the deceased owners. I wrote her a two-page letter explaining to her who we were and what we were trying to accomplish, inquiring, of course, whether the land was for sale. She sent back a kind reply that she would love to sell the place to us, but her kids, who lived in Oregon as well, wouldn't stand for it. Foiled again.

In the course of our search, we came across another empty farmstead, only this time we knew the property was available. The farm land around it was going to be auctioned off, and the 15-acre farmstead would be auctioned separately. We walked the property and noted the many mature oaks, as well as a fine barn, garage, and other outbuildings. The house wasn't much, but it was in decent condition. A low area in back of the farmstead had been drained, but probably could be restored as a pond. Our mild interest in the place soon gave way to indifference, and we pretty much forgot about it. Then one day, while I was at work, Kathy took a call from the property's owners asking if we were still interested in buying the farmstead because no one had made a bid on it in the auction, and they wanted to dispose of it quickly. Kathy said she didn't think so, and then the caller said, "Well, would you at least offer us $5,000?" Kathy told me about the call as soon as I came home that day, but neither one of us thought we should pursue the opportunity, a decision that comes back to haunt me from time to time. $5,000? Come on, that would amount to stealing the place. But we rationalized that we only had so much money, and we needed to spend it on property we really wanted. And so, we never called back. I could kick myself today because, even if we never lived there, a $5,000 investment then would have grown many times over in the years following. I suppose everyone at one time or another has let a golden, once-in-a-lifetime opportunity like this pass them by. This is not a story I have often told.

In the spring of 1993, we resumed our search for land following a winter hiatus, looking primarily in Todd County. We drove all over the eastern part of the county, rich in hills and lakes, and contacted a realty office or two, but to no avail. We just couldn't find anything that suited us, and I was wearing out after four years of getting my hopes up only to see them dashed. At some point that spring, I told Kathy that I was giving up on this business. I had had enough.

But on Sunday, May 16, while reading the Minneapolis paper as usual, I couldn't help but take a peek at the classified listings for "recreational land," as I had done many times before. There my eyes fell on an ad offering 40 acres of "woods, hills, and meadows" overlooking a pond for the sum of $12,000. Well, all bets were off, and I was back in business again in an instant. After a quick call to my boss to ask for time off, I called Chris, the owner of the 40 acres, and arranged to meet him at the property at 11 the next morning. The land was located in the heart of Minnesota's northern lake country. Chris was waiting for me when I drove up to his place, and I liked him instantly. A trim man in his late 30s with an easy manner about him, Chris owned a hundred-acre old farm that hadn't been worked in years and was selling off a 40-acre parcel on the west side of his land. "Follow me," he said. "We have to walk on over to see the property." Starting out from the farm's original building site, where only a barn remained, we hiked through a grove of trees, across a small field and down along one end of a nine-acre pond. Then, entering an extensive line of alders and hazel brush, we encountered a two-foot wide channel full of water that beavers had dug to use as part of their transportation network in the low areas surrounding the pond. Once across, we soon climbed a hill that was mostly open except for a couple of hazel clumps and a small white pine near its crest.

When I got to the top of the hill, I turned to look back. It was then that I knew our search was over. The scene then was pretty much as it is today. The hill overlooks the pond and a field in the distance. A line of trees – poplar, oak, and birch predominantly – provides a backdrop to the field, and scattered white and red pines tower above everything across the vista. A stand of paper birch marks the south edge of the hill. Near there, a small clearing between the birch and some clumps of mature ironwood (Kathy dubbed them the "Three Sisters") slopes down to a group of big oaks and jack pines. These trees form the northern boundary of another small meadow 200 yards or so in the distance. The northern slope of the main hill descends to another tiny pond surrounded by alders and small birch trees, and across this lowland a small hill covered with trees overlooks still another meadow. Facing west, I saw a forest of mostly oak and birch stretching south and west, with stands of poplar mixed in. Later, I discovered another meadow on the other side of some dense brush that eventually would be home to a pond, barn, and an orchard.

On the east side of the hill there is a beautiful mature bur oak, flanked on the right by a tall birch and a single jack pine. The three trees stand alone on the open slope, and we soon came to treasure them, referring to them as "The Trinity." The sturdy oak, with its long outstretch limbs, represents the Father, while the birch with its white bark and beautiful shimmering foliage, symbolizes the Holy Spirit. Finally, the jack pine, always green even through the white, snowy winter, represents the Son. If there is a sacred spot on our land, those three trees occupy it. That hillside with its modest, but serene view is, to us, a gift from above because it helped Kathy and me rediscover our true selves and renew our spirits.

After stopping atop the hill and taking it all in for a few minutes, Chris and I continued our trek – now mostly through the woods and thick brush. He took me to the south and west edges of the 40 that adjoin wild, uninhabited county-owned land. From those edges, we could see a couple of remote ponds and stretches of forest surrounding them. I was pleased to discover an abundance of oak and birch on the property, as well as poplar, maple, black ash, basswood, ironwood, balm of Gilead (balsam poplar), and black cherry. A township road runs the length of the northern boundary, connecting us to neighbors and town. Most of the land is high ground, although it is laced with interconnecting wetlands that provide excellent drainage. There was no question where the house would be situated – on top of the hill overlooking the pond. We wanted a site to have good drainage, a slope for a gravity flow septic system, and to be open to the south and east to benefit from the sun's warmth in winter. The latter advantage is significant. We came to learn not only the heating value of solar power, but we also grew to appreciate the pleasure of having abundant sunshine pouring in on cold winter days through windows on the east and south. Putting on some good music, kicking back the easy chair, and letting the sun warm you as you take your nap – all these things are important to consider on a homestead. The hill would give us all that, as well as provide ample room for vegetable and flower gardens. Best, the site was pretty much open, so we wouldn't have to clear brush and trees before building. The open hilltop stretches out to

after a little more discussion and a handshake, I gave Chris a $500 check as earnest money for the purchase of the forty. He thanked me, and said he would set up a closing date. After four years of searching and a lot of disappointment, frustration, and seeming futility, it was as easy as that. I was pretty happy as I got in the pickup and drove into town for a sandwich before the long ride home to deliver the big news to Kathy.

In the short time Chris and I visited, I learned some things about him. He actually lived in Bemidji and had purchased the farm a year or so earlier following a divorce. He left a good, financially-rewarding job in the pharmaceutical business and was searching for something else to do with his life. After buying the farm, he began to restore the old barn, which sits 50 yards back from the pond. Carpentry pleased him, and he took time to do the job right. In addition to making some structural improvements within, he put a new cedar shake roof on the barn and also sided it with treated boards and battens. Chris owned two llamas and fenced off a portion of a field for them. He also built a charming little barn-like shelter for the llamas within the pasture that featured an enclosed loft and outside flight of steps. Visitors to Minnesota's Itasca State Park were surprised once to see this man walking with two llamas along a trail in the park. Chris's dog, Luka, a border collie, stayed on the property when Chris was away, and he loved to climb up to the landing at the top of the llama shelter staircase to keep watch. After buying the land, we would see Chris from time to time, even after he moved away. He completed a course of study in carpentry at a technical college and became excited at the prospect of going to Africa for a year to help with construction projects organized by a church group. But as things worked out, political unrest in the African country prevented him from going, so he moved to Georgia, where his sister lived, and took a job building storage sheds for a retail home center. The last time we heard from him was at Christmas one year, when we received a card informing us that he had met and married a woman whose last name was Turgeon. We chuckle over the thought that Chris probably had never encountered a Turgeon before meeting me, and then just a few years later ends up marrying one.

The little GMC pickup hummed along nicely as I drove home after meeting Chris, and my head was abuzz with thoughts of what I had just seen and what might lie ahead. I had no doubt Kathy would be happy that we finally found a piece of property, and I was anxious to get home and tell her the exciting news.

Was I in for a surprise.

"Kathy, I found us a great piece of property and bought it," I blurted out. "I think you will really like it. It has everything we have been looking for."

"Well," she said without the slightest inflection. *That's all. Nothing more.* Just a deadpan, "Well." That astounded me because I knew exactly the meaning of this response. It wasn't the first time I'd heard it in the course of our marriage. It's a totally noncommittal answer, a reply that doesn't want to offend, but at the same time makes sure there is no trace of enthusiasm or support for whatever idea is being presented. From this, you are to draw all necessary meaning and take heed of it. I have a good friend who has his own way of delivering this kind of message. He simply says, "Uh-huh." You can come up with a great idea, but all you get in return is, "Well" or "Uh-huh"!

Now, if anything was going to deflate me over the purchase of this property, Kathy's little noncommittal "well" was sure to do it. I needed something more than that. I needed to hear her say, "Great!" or "Super!" or even "Sounds like a good deal, honey." I don't remember where the conversation went from there, but I probably wasn't listening anyway. Yet, I wasn't angry. Without her on board, all I could think about was how I was going to get out of this mess. It soon was bedtime, and I was tired after the long, hectic day, but sleep eluded me. As I tossed and turned, I knew I had to ask Chris for our money back, and that's what I proposed to Kathy, who said it was OK with her. The next morning finally came, and feeling depleted and depressed, I made a call to Chris before going to work, asking to have my earnest money returned because we just couldn't go through with the deal. He couldn't have been more gracious and said he'd send the check back that day. When I kept apologizing, he said, "Bill, it's just a land deal." I will always remember his kindness.

That was on Tuesday. By Wednesday, after a good sleep the night before, my relief at getting out of the commitment with Chris began to erode, and soon I was a wreck again, thinking, "What have I done? This is what I want! We're going to let this slip away, and then we won't have anything." Pathetic as it appears, that's the way it was, and I was pretty much in turmoil for the rest of the day, impatient to talk with Kathy that evening after work.

It didn't take much conversing to understand that Kathy also was having second thoughts, and before long I was back on the phone telling Chris of our change of heart and wondering whether we could meet him Saturday morning so she could look at the property. Of course, by then my original check was on its way back to me in the mail. Chris said, sure, he would meet us, so on Saturday we made the trip as planned. When Kathy ascended the hill overlooking the pond, she, too, knew this was the place we had been looking for, and within an hour we had given Chris another check for the earnest money. We then drove into town, where we had a long lunch at the local cafe, riding high on our positive thoughts about what the future might bring now that, at last, we had a piece of land, a future homestead – a place to focus our energies on for years to come.

On the way home that afternoon, I felt confident enough to bring up our shaky handling of the land purchase, asking Kathy why she didn't show more enthusiasm when first informed of the deal. I told her I was looking for any kind of positive feedback so that I would know I had done the right thing. It was exasperating to learn she was looking for the same thing from me. "You just didn't look very excited about it, like you

3

Cutting Out the Road Ahead

In December 1992, months before we put down the earnest money on our land, I bought a new red GMC Sonoma pickup, not because I thought I was going to need one up north, but mainly because it was handy to have one to haul things. Besides, most of my friends at work drove pickups, and I was tired of calling on them when I needed to transport something or asking them to let me use their trailers. The compact-size pickup, the smallest made by GMC, would serve me well, I thought, so I was surprised at the friendly ribbing I took when I announced my purchase to co-workers at coffee one day in the college's student union. My pickup had two-wheel drive and a standard cab, and everyone, they assured me, knows that four-wheel drive with extended cab is better, not only for traversing difficult terrain or plowing through snow, but also for resale. Well, I really didn't think of all that when I bought the vehicle, and, besides, the four-wheelers were more expensive. Soon they christened me "Basic Bill," a guy who goes after the minimum, who always chooses the stripped-down version when there is a better choice. From previous conversations, they knew I subscribed to the basic cable TV plan in town, so they all had a good laugh in coming up with my new name.

I don't know if their assessment of me was on target or whether I lived up to the name in the years ahead, but I can say that it fit into my notion of homesteading. I bought used items when I could find them and tried to fix or improve them. Over time, I became a good scrounger, always looking to make something out of things other people discard. Yet, I also learned that with certain items, like a chainsaw, one should buy the best available. That's what I did, buying a Swedish-made saw that has served me exceedingly well for many years now and has never been in the repair shop.

As soon as we made the deal for the land and began to think about cutting out trees for a driveway, it became obvious that we were tool-deficient and ill-equipped to undertake the array of tasks before us. So the chainsaw became an urgent item on a long list of things we would need. A second, even more critical, need was a camper. We needed a place to sleep and cook our meals when we were at the property. On one of our trips north that spring, I noticed a pop-up tent camper with a for-sale sign on it in the same little town where we would take shelter during the storm four years later. The Apache tent camper seemed in decent shape. The seller had pulled out the sides and set up the tent, but, truthfully, I didn't look at it closely. The $300 price seemed fair, so I bought it and happily towed it home with my pickup. There, I rolled it into the back yard and pulled out the sides to set up the tent and secure the door. To our dismay, Kathy and I discovered the tent had a lot of holes, but, true to herself, she took to mending them as best she could. That's the way she is, always trying to make the best of what she is given. Although the camper challenge was steep, her willingness to spruce up second-hand goods benefited us in the years ahead. As I examined the camper, it became apparent that it was too basic even for Basic Bill. It had a table, but no sink or stove, and the zip-up door and plastic used to line the screens on the sides were shabby. One of our neighbors who came for a look was aghast when we told her of our plans to sleep in the Apache. "There are bears

would not stand up to heavy use. How wrong they were. The trailer has fiberglass sides, but its aluminum framing and edging make it nearly indestructible, even when I fill it with a load of heavy oak firewood. Best, it is lightweight and easy to maneuver by hand when hooking up to a vehicle or tractor. It was of great help hauling all sorts of things to our property, and over the years became a workhorse on our place, hauling not only firewood, but also brush, sand, manure, straw bales, compost, and all sorts of building materials.

Finding something to replace the Apache didn't take long. We bought a used 19-foot, hard-top camper for $1,100. Kathy enjoyed cleaning the inside from top to bottom, making new curtains for it, and generally trying her best to make it as homey as possible. This would be our home away from home for many weekends.

The property closing was scheduled for July 9, but I made a trip north in early June just to walk the land again and take a closer look. I'm glad I did because I discovered that the main hill where I knew our house would one day be situated was not fully within the confines of the 40 acres. The building site sat in the extreme northeast corner of the forty, but the property line there cut directly across the lower end of the long eastern slope and would be unacceptably close to the house and yard, particularly since the septic system would likely run in that direction. This became an instant concern, so I walked back through the woods to the township road, where my truck was parked, and headed over to see Chris. He came by and saw the problem, so we worked out a deal for me to buy three more acres on the northeast corner of the forty at an additional cost of $1,500. Most of the three acres was low, brushy and wet, but the extra land guaranteed a much larger and workable building site.

When the closing day came, Kathy and I thought we were ready to start our first project – cutting out a swath through the woods for our driveway. I had walked through this section numerous times to determine the best route, but in reality there was only one way to go: Follow a ridge curving around a small tamarack wetland that gradually ascended to the main hill. This suited us perfectly because my brother, Jerry, had told me to make sure we put a curve in the driveway so that no one on the township road could see all way to the top. As it turned out, the driveway enters the property between two low areas, curves left and then cuts back to the right before reaching an open area near the top of the hill.

All we had to do was cut down the trees and clear the brush away. My chainsaw was ready, and I had rented a hand-held brush cutter, one of those noisy, smoky, weed-whip contraptions with a circular saw blade that I quickly learned to hate. When we had signed the closing papers, Chris asked us what we were planning to do next. Kathy said we were going to cut down the trees for the driveway, yet neither one of us could say yes when Chris asked if we had ever done anything like this before. "I'd better come out there and give you a hand," he said. It didn't take him long to knock over about 30 trees with his chainsaw, while I used the brush cutter ahead of him to cut a path and establish the general direction of the road. I then began using my chainsaw to cut limbs off the trees that Chris fell. Things were going quite well until I attempted to cut down a half-dead oak near the top of the road. I made the proper cuts on each side of the tree, causing it to fall where intended, but, unfortunately, the tree crashed down on top of the rented brush cutter, which I had set down and forgotten about in my zeal to become a lumberjack. The brush cutter broke in half and resembled a dead snake when I picked it up. Late that afternoon, I walked into the rental place to return the broken cutter and was thank-

mauve-flowered milkweed were showing off their stuff, and we strolled past clumps of tall birches, down a hill and under the twisting, outstretched limbs of a pair of big bur oaks. We stopped to watch a grey squirrel scamper up a tree and gazed at the blue sky.

It was then that I rediscovered something from my youth – the common mullein. Considered a weed, it was used as a medicinal herb for treating coughs and diarrhea, and it grows most anywhere the soil has been disturbed. It often comes up after gophers dig up the ground or when new garden space is cultivated. Mullein is a biennial plant, growing only low rosettes of soft, large bluish-green leaves the first year, then sending out a tall stalk with a long, flowering spike the next year. Flowers appear on the spike all summer long, but only in certain places at any given time. The spike is never in full bloom. Mullein was also called torch plant or miner's candle because its head can be dipped in oil and lighted for use as a torch. Mullein seeds can stay buried in the ground for a hundred years, and the plant must have full sunshine to grow. I remember the mullein as a common plant where I grew up, but forgot about it entirely in later years. It is a rare sight in heavily-farmed areas these days, but in the lake country of Minnesota any disturbed soil will soon produce the common mullein. I think the mullein is a metaphor for those of us who have struggled to find identity in our lives. Personal growth sometimes does not occur until we first experience trials that disturb our complacency and expose us to reality. And like the mullein, we may not bloom the first year, but instead struggle on and only later begin to show our true colors, a little at a time. And so, I have come to hold the mullein in high esteem, for it has shown me that the pain and sadness of the past can lead to understanding and growth.

It was during these walks that we came to call our place Hiram Hill. Nothing is more natural than to give your little piece of ground a name, I think. We didn't have to debate the subject long, but picked the name Hiram because it was the first name of an early settler in the area and, actually, the alliteration appealed to us. We also noted a Biblical connection. King Hiram of Tyre in Lebanon sent architects, workmen, and cedar timbers to King Solomon of Israel for building the first temple in Jerusalem. That next winter, we carefully studied the many pictures we took on walks and drew a colorful little map of Hiram Hill, anticipating the location of the house, shop, garden, woodshed, and orchard. Surprisingly, much of the map is still accurate today.

Strenuous, repetitive tasks can be enjoyable – it all depends on your attitude. We found that out while picking up brush and tree limbs on the side of our road after it was built in mid-September. We had already cut off the limbs on the trees, but nothing was picked up, including the trees themselves, which we cut into lengths for firewood and stacked nearby under two big red oaks. There was a great amount of brush and limbs to pick up, and we had to make dozens of trips up and down the road with the pickup and trailer. Once we had a load, we went to the top of the hill and made a big pile for burning later. This took several weekends of work in October, but we remember those days fondly. For the most part, the weather was quite beautiful that fall, and we would tackle one big pile of brush after another until we grew tired and took a break, maybe stopping to eat a sandwich and tossing a bite to Kirby, our dog, who was always nearby. Kathy would hear my story about how my dad would send me off to plow a 50-acre field with a small Ford tractor and a two-bottom plow. I would say, "Dad, I'll never get done." But he would reply, "Son, if you go around the field enough times, you'll get it done."

Kathy, in turn, would chide me for working so fast – jumping in hard, but tiring quickly. We concluded that she is slow, but steady, while I am fast and – not so steady. But together we made a good team, and our days of picking up the brush and tree cuttings will always be precious ones, working side by side, making something better and just enjoying the pleasure of good, honest work in the crisp autumn air.

By the third weekend of October, the road's edges looked reasonably tidy, and Jack, our road builder, had spread a thick layer of good-grade gravel on it. The grass that we had sown in mid-September had already started to appear. I took the time to put together a good pasture mix of grass seed, and when I planted it in September, I made sure I generously scattered the seed. Of course, I planted far more seeds than needed, for in the spring, the grass was almost too thick to grow properly. Kathy was not surprised at this, of course, because she knows that with me if one is good, two have to be even better. She has rolled her eyes more than once watching me work, making statements like, "Honey, if you give that nut just one more turn, you might be able to break it off." Well, even so, the grass looked great the next year, and we could pride ourselves on all the hard work we had put in the previous fall.

Once the road was built, we were able to tow the camper from Chris's property to the top of the hill, where we parked it next to some birch trees in a spot that would be occupied by our shop/cabin the next summer. We didn't get electricity until mid-October, but once it was available, it allowed us to stay in the camper even on cold nights. A blacksmith shop back home constructed a gate that I had designed, and after a couple of false starts, we finally got the posts installed and the gate in place. We thought this would be a good thing, but I have told other newcomers to the area in recent years not to put in a gate. All it does is advertise that someone isn't home. We learned this lesson more than once in the years ahead, as thieves cut the chain locking the gate and stole our belongings.

It was late October, and we already had made nine trips to and from the property since I first visited the place in May. Our little pickup was performing admirably and would make the trip approximately 84 more times before we moved there permanently. I kept track of every trip, writing down the things we did and the people we met. When it was all over, I calculated the following based on the total number of round trips that one or both of us made during the period from 1993 to 1997:

Total Number of Trips: 93

Total Miles: 40,920 (440 per round trip)

Total Gallons of Gas (based on 20 mpg): 2,046

Total Cost (based on $1.20 per gallon): $2,455.20

Only once would I have benefited from having a four-wheel drive pickup – when we tried to back the camper into its place for winter. Otherwise, we got along just fine without it and appreciated the better gas mileage a two-wheeler generally chalks up. Call me Basic Bill, if you want.

Kathy didn't accompany me on the last trip that first year, and this became sort of the custom in the next several years. By the last weekend of October, the weather usually is quite cold, but I always wanted to run up there one more time to check things out before winter really set in. And so that first year I drove up on the last Saturday to post some no-hunting signs in preparation for the upcoming deer hunt. Most years, a neighbor or friend would hunt on our land, but I hadn't yet made any arrangements.

A dusting of snow covered the ground and the sky was overcast and gray, but I was captivated by the silence and solitude of the moment and decided to take a walk. Heading through a thicket of hazel that leads to the west meadow, where our barn would stand someday, I saw an opening in the woods among some small oaks and birch. Entering there and working my way through a brush-free area, I soon found myself climbing a steep, tree-covered hill. The hill rises higher than any in the immediate area, but doesn't stand out when summer's leafy canopy keeps it concealed. Several big oaks stand on the top, and it provides a good view of the terrain all around it, especially after the leaves have fallen. I christened it, "Hidden Hill." It was one of the things we added to the map we drew that winter, and it is still a favorite place of mine when the dogs and I head out on our trails.

As I continued my walk under the dull sky, I went over to a place we have come to call "Beaver Point," a small hill overlooking a tiny pond and meadow to the north of the main hill. There, beaver recently had toppled a half-dozen or so poplars, hauling the branches to their lodge on the main pond to use as food during the winter. The next spring we would come back there and cut up the trees they left behind for firewood. Beaver Point is also a favorite of ours, for it provides a wonderful view to the southeast across the big pond, and a cluster of chokecherry bushes sits in the meadow it overlooks.

My steps also took me south to a clutch of woods we call "Birch Arbor." There, huge, 50-foot high birches rise up on a slope, with only a scattering of small ironwood trees below them. Heavily shaded and free of brush, the forest floor in summer becomes a carpet of thin, lacey grass and balsam leaves beneath the slanted white columns of the birches. On hot, sunny days in the summer, Birch Arbor is a cool, green, moist oasis for me and the dogs.

Making my way back to the camper and checking things one more time, I stood by the pickup in the gray stillness and felt the cold air pinch my cheeks. It was time to say goodbye, and I took a last look across the pond at the quiet landscape. Chris's handsome, restored barn and the towering white pine behind it stood as sentinels in the disappearing light. Sleep, Hiram Hill, I thought. Sleep 'til our return.

4

A Plan for the Future

For Sale: Used windows.
Various sizes, with attached
aluminum storms. Good
condition, reasonable.

When I saw the ad in the supermarket advertiser that I had picked up on the way home after work, I immediately called the number and asked if I could take a look at the windows. It was dark when Kathy and I arrived at the seller's country home near town. He said he had replaced the windows in his house the previous summer, and the old ones were stacked in the farm's empty granary. Climbing over a huge snowdrift that had been hardened by southwestern Minnesota's persistent winds, we entered the granary and found a stack of five serviceable windows that would fit nicely in our plans for the shop/cabin we intended to build the next spring on Hiram Hill. As we agreed on a price of $75 for the lot, I noticed a circulator-type wood stove sitting nearby and asked about it. "I'll let you have it for $25," the young man said. I looked it over and told him he had a deal. We struggled to carry out the heavy windows with their wooden frames over the big snow bank, but soon they were stacked in the back of the GMC. The seller worked in town and told me he would clean up the stove and bring it to me, which he did a couple of days later. The Wonderwood stove actually had not been used all that much, and it became a fixture in our shop/cabin. Browsing in a farm supply store years later, I saw a new Wonderwood for sale there with a price tag of $500.

Winter became a time for us to plan, gather, and build what we would need to create a homestead on Hiram Hill. I suppose it's that way for anyone who has a getaway in a northern climate. The seasons dictate the flow of activity, and they probably increase the pleasure of it all. As winters drag on, owners long to get back to their cabins, woods, and lakes, and when they eventually get to return, they savor each precious day. And so it was with us. Most of our free time in winter centered on Hiram Hill-related activities. We read books and maga-

the next summer, even though it would take us until the spring of 1995 to completely finish the interior. Friends and family wanted to visit, and we needed a place for them to stay. We wanted something that would serve as a cabin, but later could be used as a shop and garage, once we built a house. Wonderful ideas raced through our minds and became the focus of our conversations, but the hard reality of finances made sure we kept our senses. I especially was interested in a carriage-style structure with a salt-box roof that featured living space on the second floor, but it would prove too costly to contemplate seriously. Eventually, we settled on a 24-by-28 foot framed building that we could insulate and finish ourselves. The windows we had bought, along with a masonry chimney we planned to construct, would give the structure the appearance of a small house or cabin.

Once we made our decision to build, we needed to begin assembling things to furnish it and make it a home. In my basement work space during the 1993-94 and 1994-95 winters, I built a set of Adirondack chairs, including a loveseat; a chest for storage; a set of cabinets and a large workbench that would serve as our "kitchen" counter; a firewood box; a kindling box; a vanity with a recycled bathroom sink; a wall divider; a sled

sel fuel, a box of matches, and a pitchfork – items we would need to burn the brush. Arriving around 10, we stopped first at the fire warden's house to ask permission to burn. We really didn't need to ask because the snow cover was more than adequate, but I didn't want to take any chances. The fire warden, a long-time local resident, just smiled and said, "Light 'er up." We parked at the entrance to our road and got ready to walk up. After climbing over a snow bank created by the road plows and stepping around our gate, which was pretty much buried in snow, we happily pulled our sled up the driveway. The brush pile was covered with a couple feet of snow, but I was able to remove most of it by lifting away sections with my hands. This took a half-hour to accomplish, and I was anxious to start burning. I found a spot with small limbs and hazel brush that I thought might catch fire quickly and stuffed wads of newspaper beneath the cuttings. After soaking everything liberally with diesel fuel, I lit a match and tossed it into the newspaper. The paper began to burn quite rapidly and the branches seemed to catch fire, but once the newspaper was consumed, the brush smoldered for a bit and then gave out altogether. A second and third attempt failed as well, and I knew we needed to do something else.

Down the snowy driveway we went, heading over to see Fred, a farmer, who lived just down the road about a mile. Fred had lived all his life in the area, knew most everyone, and I figured I should ask him for advice. Fred would become a good friend of ours in the coming years and give us many wonderful memories. After I explained our predicament, Fred took me to his barn, where he handed me a bundle of twine saved from hay bales and some pine-tree pitch. Pitch is a resinous deposit found in old pine tree stumps, and it burns intensely when lit. Fred told me to put down the newspaper, twine and pitch, soak it with a little diesel fuel, and light it. The pitch would ignite and keep burning for a long time, hopefully long enough to get a good fire going in the pile. He also told me in the future to put a piece of tarp over a small section of the pile to keep it dry until it's time to burn, placing the tarp on the northwest corner because in winter, the prevailing breeze is from the northwest and would help fan the flames.

Back to our place we went, grateful to Fred for this counsel. It was only about half past 11, so we still had plenty of time to burn. I placed the newspaper, twine, and pitch as Fred instructed, poured on some diesel fuel, and lit a match. The flames took off as before, but now the pitch caught fire and kept the flames going until the brush ignited. Soon we had a big fire going, and its roar increased as it spread to the entire pile. Kathy and I sat on the sled at the top of the slope, watching the fire and feeling the heat on our cheeks. It was a splendid day, with a deep blue cloudless sky and a light breeze from the northwest. In a couple of hours most of the brush and branches had been consumed, but I worked my way around the fire with my pitchfork, digging out pieces on the edge that were covered with snow and throwing them in the fire. Taking breaks, I would just lean on my pitchfork and watch the flames do their work. It was a pleasant task, really, and we would repeat it every year for many years. We now have a burning site in the meadow by Beaver Point, and brush, branches, tree limbs, and garden refuse are hauled there for burning each winter.

Times like these give us pause for reflection, I think. The burning of a brush pile is a sort of passage rite to me, a step forward that puts the past behind and allows us to tackle what is before us. Perhaps we should all "burn" the brush piles of disappointment, failures, and mistakes that mark the past instead of letting them be obstacles in our paths forward. As the fire warden said, light 'er up!

As time passed, I was becoming increasingly aware that careful planning would be a necessity if we were to make things work as we built our homestead. More than once we would arrive up north only to find that we didn't have the right tools or materials for the job. I learned to take a few minutes to think through a job step by step so that I knew exactly what I would need. Lists of things to do became a big part of my life, and sometimes they were so long they became intimidating. Later, after we moved to Hiram Hill permanently, I would make seasonal lists. Writing down the broader goals for our place also became important, and they often were the focal points of our discussions in the evenings. In the summer of 1993, not long after purchasing the property, I sat down and drew up the following plan:

1993

Improvements

Install road, install power, put up gate

Activities

Clear out trees, clean up brush, burn brush, plant grass along road

Equipment Needed

Camper, chainsaw, trailer

1994

Improvements

Build wood shed, install horseshoe pits, build compost bins

Activities

Split wood from road, plant trees, plant fruit trees, clear brush, mow meadows

Equipment Needed

Splitting maul, carpentry tools, tractor, brush cutter for tractor

1995

Improvements

Build shop/cabin, put in phone, build footbridge

Activities

Cut/split more wood, put in garden, cut out trails, plant tree seedlings

Equipment Needed

Snow blower for tractor, fishing boat and motor

1996

Improvements

Dig well, build root cellar

Activities

Maintain garden, meadows, trails

Equipment Needed

4-wheel drive vehicle

1997

Improvements

Build house

1998

Enjoy Hiram Hill

The plan was something of a stretch for me at the time because I just didn't foresee a lot of things. We dug our well in 1995 rather than 1996 because we absolutely were tired of hauling gallon jugs of water from home to get us through the weekends. And we needed a better form of shelter than the camper provided, so we built the cabin in 1994, not 1995, as I had envisioned. And some things on the list never materialized, such as the fishing boat and motor. The footbridge would be built later in a different location than originally planned, and the root cellar would become instead a cold storage cabinet in our basement. Finally, a 4-wheel drive pickup didn't become a reality until 2003. Nonetheless, the list provided a general framework for us to proceed and would be modified as time when on. But a general "Hiram Hill Plan" would always be in place to guide us.

The long winter finally came to an end, and we were impatient to move things forward. During one of two visits in April, we lined up Jack, the man who built our road, to prepare the site for the cabin. He wouldn't be able to get to that until the end of May. But still we came, making the trip every weekend in May, and doing things like cutting brush back from the edges of the open areas and clearing a path to the west meadow. We also planted a couple of lilac bushes that we managed to forget about. Then one May years later, we noticed them in full bloom next to some alders that had grown up around them.

But there was one pressing need, and Kathy kept reminding me: We needed to install an outhouse on the property. We were the only residents in the immediate area, and the closest neighbor was nearly mile away. So, with privacy easy to come by, we just took care of business the best we could and used the camper toilet sparingly. But with friends and family wanting to come and see the property, we needed an outhouse. In the lake country, outhouses are a common thing, and lumber yards have pre-built ones made of cedar or pine lined up for sale outside their stores. We selected a longer-lasting, cedar one-hole model that cost a little more, but proved to be a good choice when we eventually converted it to a garden tool shed. After loading it in our

Apache trailer, we headed out to Hiram Hill, where I immediately grabbed a shovel and dug a hole between some poplars in back of where our shop/cabin would be built. We soon had the outhouse in place. To mark the occasion, I took a picture of Kathy and Kirby sitting on the outhouse seat with the door wide open, and the photo hangs in our bathroom today as evidence of the progress we've made since those days.

When the cabin was constructed, I put floodlights on the side facing the privy so users wouldn't be in the dark when nature called at night. But we found out some of our guests dreaded using the outhouse, even a clean, new one like ours with fresh paint. It was always a major concern of our daughter when she visited us from Boston. She would be in and out in seconds. Once, though, she opened the door and a squirrel greeted her by darting out. She let out a scream worthy of a bear, and we all came running, thinking the worst, then had a good chuckle. I'll give her credit, though – she bravely continued to use our humble facility, but approached it warily, always fearing the worst.

Showering was another concern, but we solved that by buying a solar shower bag that you fill with water, put in the sun for heating, and then hang from above for showering. It worked beautifully. Private as we were, we could take showers in the open. We had moved the camper to the top of the hill so it wouldn't be in the way when the site was prepared for the shop/cabin. I hung the shower bag from a board fastened on top of the camper and had a slatted platform on the ground to stand on. There, we would shower in broad daylight high on our hill overlooking the pond and the fields in the distance. Later, I lashed a 2x4 between two trees in the woods and hung the shower bag there, clearing out a path and space and putting down a bench to sit on and the slatted platform to stand on, as well. That gave our guests a bit of privacy, but definitely hurried them along if mosquitoes or black flies decided to join them in this woodsy accommodation. My sister, Alyce, ever the good sport, gamely showered there when she visited us and asked Kathy to take a picture of her showering, her modesty fully safeguarded by the dense foliage surrounding her. She put the photo on her Christmas card that year. Still later, in our never-ending quest to upgrade our facilities, we hung the water bag from a beam in our newly-built wood shed and placed a shower curtain in front for privacy.

Things soon began to happen quickly. Jack hauled

in sand to make a level site for the shop/cabin, and 10 days later workmen put in a concrete slab and laid down a single course of block around the perimeter of the slab. Then in a matter of a few days, Kevin, our carpenter, and his helper framed and roofed the building and installed the doors and windows. The wiring and construction of the chimney would be done later. In addition, Kathy and I would install the insulation and interior walls, but that work didn't start until fall and wasn't completed until the next spring. In the meantime, we had a myriad of other jobs to get done – painting trim, moving dirt with a tractor I had purchased, installing patio blocks for a walkway, adding screen doors, and the like. We worked long hours to get everything done. One memory that sticks came after we had landscaped the ground surrounding the building and seeded it to grass. We purchased some bales of straw from Fred, our neighbor, and then spread the straw over the seeded areas. By six o'clock the job was finished, and as I walked up the incline near the cabin heading to our camper, exhausted and ready to call it a day, my pants suddenly fell to my knees. Kathy had come out to tell me it was time to eat and witnessed this little spectacle, much to her delight.

With the shop that would serve as our cabin now a reality, we could leave the camper and begin staying inside the building, even though it was just an empty shell with no ceiling and the wiring exposed. But we had a place to sleep and could plug in the electric stove and refrigerator. We used a picnic table to eat on. For our bed, we pushed two folding cots together over which we placed a foam mattress salvaged from the Apache tent camper.

No longer having a need for the hard-shell camper, I thought I would try to sell it, but fortunately a fellow who delivered some of the building materials for the shop/cabin solved that situation. As part of his duties at the lumber yard, he built storage sheds. In the course of our conversations, he mentioned to me that each year he and his wife attended WE Fest, a country music jamboree, but didn't think they would go this year because their old camper had seen its better days. A light went on in my head, and I asked him if he would build me a storage shed in exchange for the camper. He jumped at the opportunity, and in a couple of weeks he drove up to our place with an 8x10-foot shed on a trailer, which he unloaded in a spot I had prepared. Later, he and his wife came back for the camper, and the two of them took it to WE Fest each year. He framed the shed using two-by-fours sawed on his dad's portable mill, and as an employee of the lumber yard, he bought the other materials at a discount. Country bartering at its best, I thought. The cabin was our place to live and sleep, and we needed a shed to store shovels, garden hoses, gasoline, and the like.

So there we were, with two buildings on the property already. We had decided on gray vinyl siding for the shop/cabin. It followed that each subsequent building would be painted gray, except for the house, which also was sided with gray vinyl, and the barn – built a good many years later – which would be stained New England barn red. The decision to use vinyl on the shop/cabin and house didn't come easily, as I resisted strenuously, saying I wanted something more natural like cedar or pine that we could paint or stain. Kathy never wavered in her resistance to this idea, looking ahead to the not-too-distant future when we were older and likely would dread having to scrap away peeling paint and put on a new coat. She won the argument, and in retrospect I am glad she did, because it indeed will be enough to repaint the smaller sheds on the property and re-stain the barn as the need arises. When you decide to start a homestead from scratch at 50, such decisions make sense.

But I didn't lose all the few major arguments we had. When I first walked up the hill to look at the property, I noticed a small white pine near the top. It was about three feet tall, and its "mother" undoubtedly was a beautiful 60-foot-high white pine 500 yards away to the southeast on another hilly point overlooking the beaver pond. Immediately, I thought that the little tree was perfectly situated if we built a house on the hill, and I made a mental note of it. Kathy never bought into this idea and thought it should be removed, but I resisted and made sure that when we marked the location of the house for the excavators that the tree would be saved. Today, the tree is flourishing and is taller than our house, its growth enhanced, I think, because its roots are close to the septic drain field. If Kathy ever mentions her vinyl siding triumph, I just remind her to take a look at the big, beautiful white pine outside our window.

Cutting out road, July 1993.

A brush pile takes shape, October 1993.

Kathy unloading firewood, October 1993.

Shop/cabin and wood shed, Fall 1994.

Shop/cabin living room and kitchen, 1995.

Bill digging out rocks on newly created trails, 1996.

Hauling in firewood.

Dragline in early stages of digging pond, 2001.

5

CHASING COWS AND DREAMS

O ur days on Hiram Hill began to be less hectic as we settled into our makeshift quarters in the cabin shell and welcomed family and friends who wanted to see our place. Our homesteading adventure was in its infancy, and we were just trying to come up with a reasonable shelter and a few conveniences. Homesteading as we envisioned it would come later, when we could plant gardens, start an orchard, put up food, and raise chickens and pigs. We hardly were set up to receive anyone, but we did the best we could, and those who stayed overnight had to sleep on cots or foam mattresses, use the outhouse, and forgo regular showers. Some brought their own campers. Our meals weren't fancy, but they were entirely adequate for the conditions, or so we thought. The area we are located in draws many tourists because of the woods and lakes and boasts an

71

array of recreational pursuits, so we took our visitors biking, hiking, canoeing, and boating. They took in flea markets and visited state parks, as well as just enjoyed taking a walk around our property and down our country roads.

Black flies, deer flies, mosquitoes, and wood ticks also enthusiastically welcomed our visitors. In northern Minnesota, black flies are worst than mosquitoes, in my opinion, and sometimes seemed to swarm on anyone intent on enjoying the great outdoors. Some days you could see a squadron or two of them hovering over my head and the dogs as we journeyed down the gravel road. Now, I place a feather in my cap in a desperate hope that the flies will congregate at the tip of the feather rather than at the hole in the back of my baseball cap. Most of the time a breeze keeps the pests away. But my daughter, Amanda, swears that as we rode my Ford tractor down the road one day, a group of the little devils followed just behind my head, no matter how fast we went. By then she had become more accustomed to black flies. Not so the first time she visited the property. She was living in Boston at the time and came to Minnesota for a wedding in the family. After the event, she followed Kathy and me to Hiram Hill in her rental car on her way back

we usually discovered this when we saw them down by our place. We would call Fred immediately, and then go after the cows, which invariably ran the other way and, worse, disappeared into the woods in a flash. It always amazes me how an 800-pound beast like that can slip into the dense undergrowth of the woods so deftly and be next to impossible to locate just seconds later. "Where did they go?" we would ask. Once, the cows got loose late in the evening, and after an hour of futilely chasing them in the woods and hoping to get them steered toward the township road, it became dark. My brother-in-law, Shannon, and I had a hard time finding our own way back. Fred, never one to get very excited about such things, told us the cows probably would return to the road on their own by morning. He was right. We found them early the next day about three-fourths of a mile further down the road, standing there bawling and apparently ready to end their little summertime getaway. Fred came prepared with a wooden box with feed in it and a rope attached. He dragged the box behind him as he started down the road for home, and the cows immediately began to follow. Shannon and I held up the rear of this bucolic parade, and I will never forget the scene: Fred, walking 20 or 30 feet ahead of the cows, saying "Come, boss. Come, boss." The beasts lumbered behind, their bellies swaying from side to side as they slowly made their way home in the cool and green of the early midsummer morning.

We also took our visitors berry picking when the season was right. Wild raspberries grow everywhere, and there was a big stand on our hill. Kathy would make jam with our bounty, and although we grow our own raspberries now in the garden, the wild variety make the best jam and have the most beautiful red color you can imagine. Chokecherries, too, are plentiful most years, and we learned to make syrup with them for pancakes using my mother's recipe. Hazel bushes grow everywhere, providing a good food source for squirrels and chipmunks, and occasionally we competed with the critters for the nuts, which we put in a gunny sack to dry in the sun atop the roof of our little storage shed. The drying process takes a month or so before you can remove the husks and crack the shells. The nuts are small compared to the store variety, but my ancestors loved them in *crème au sucre,* a French-Canadian dessert made of brown sugar and cream. In the fall, we also loved to search the nearby bogs for cranberries. Some years they are plentiful, some not. Whenever we find some, we put them in plastic bags for freezing to use at Thanksgiving, Christmas, and other special days. For the most part, I think our visitors those first years enjoyed their stays at Hiram Hill, rustic as they were, and came to appreciate our homesteading venture. Or, maybe they thought we were crazy.

Our life that second summer took on a certain cadence, I suppose, and we went through the work week always mindful that Friday night or, in most cases, Saturday morning meant jumping in the GMC and resuming our homestead dream. All week long we prepared for what we planned to do. Food was a critical matter, especially when we expected visitors. We also had to plan for whatever work we intended to do. That meant assembling the right tools and materials, unless we could purchase the latter at the local hardware store and lumber yard. The little Apache trailer sat in our backyard until Friday evening, when I would start loading it with things I had bought or made. Until we had our well dug, Kathy filled a couple dozen plastic jugs with water for drinking, bathing, and washing dishes. The jugs then had to be loaded, as well as our clothes, bedding, and food for the dog.

We made the trip to and from our place so many

times that we came to know the roads, towns, and scenery extremely well. For the most part, we took the same route, and we had favorite places to stop for bathroom breaks. Kathy always prepared us something to eat while en route – ham sandwiches, carrot and celery sticks, apples, and cookies. If we left early on Saturday morning, I made sure we had a supply of sugar and cinnamon-covered donuts from the local supermarket to go along with hard-boiled eggs and coffee. Kathy knew that I would be calling for the donuts even before we hit the city limits, and that I would consume an egg or two and my first cup of coffee before we reached the next sizable town, just 30 minutes away. That's why the Food N Fuel convenience store there became the first of the bathroom stops we made on our way up.

Long-suffering Kathy put up with this business with remarkably good cheer. After all, our 20-pound not-so-mini-dachshund always sat on her lap in our little pickup cab, and the bag of donuts, sandwiches, coffee thermos, water jug, and her purse covered the floor at her feet. It was always a struggle to pour the coffee – and the cream I *must* have in it. But she endured all this, I think, because I would put in a cassette tape of *Les Misérables* and down the road we would go, slurping our coffee, munching donuts, and singing, *"Master of the house, keeper of the zoo, ready to relieve them of a sou or two."*

We also made it a habit of stopping in a little town to use its park restroom and let Kirby have a run. After this stop, we pretty much took county roads the rest of the way, and this meant that there weren't any restrooms to accommodate us – except for the great outdoors. I've discovered that the farther north you go, the better chance you have of just pulling over and letting it go, without having to worry about a car zooming over the hill ahead or being too close to a farmstead. I could never make it to Hiram Hill without one more call from nature. Vern, a farmer in the Flint Hills of Kansas, once said to me, "Show me a man driving down a gravel road in a pickup truck, and I'll show you a guy who's got to stop and take a pee."

The most memorable trip to Hiram Hill occurred in 1997, about a month before we actually moved there permanently. It was late May, and the school year had ended, with Kathy saying her goodbyes to the teachers and students at the rural school where she had taught for 16 years. When she came home, she told me that a relative of one of her students had some baby pigs for us, and she said we would take them. The piglets were

our neighbors might take a couple or maybe even three. There wasn't any time to worry about it. In a few days we were going to drive up for the long Memorial Day weekend, and the little pigs would be joining us for the ride north. That Saturday morning we arrived early at the farm and loaded the five piglets inside the pickup's topper. I had created a small space in the corner of the pickup box up against the cab and filled it with shredded paper, the only bedding I could come up with at the time. I made sure the pigs couldn't climb over the sides, but that really wasn't a concern because the topper was crammed with stuff we were taking north as part of our ongoing move. Fortunately, the topper had side doors, so I partially propped them open to assure that the pigs would stay cool during the long ride. In addition to the tightly-packed topper, I was pulling the Apache trailer, also fully loaded. A friend told us that a farmer he knew had a stack of hog panels he might sell because he didn't raise pigs anymore. I ended up buying five of the 16-foot flexible panels, which I would use later to build a pen. I had to bend the panels over so they would fit into the trailer and over the other items. The panels gave the trailer the appearance of a covered wagon. And so, down the road we went with the five squealing pigs.

When we finally arrived at Hiram Hill, I immediately blocked off one of the wood shed stalls with the hog panels and put down the shredded computer paper for bedding. Thinking this was going to be a piece of cake, I opened the topper door and grabbed the first piglet to carry it to the pen. Much to my dismay, the little critter pooped all over the front of my shirt, leaving me to curse and complain while running as fast as I could to the pen. "You just had to say yes, didn't you?" I complained to Kathy. "I mean, we are trying to build a house here, and now I've got to deal with this." Fortunately, our neighbors across the pond happily took three of the pigs off our hands, so I soon forgot the little assault on my dignity and learned to love pigs. They would become part of our homestead each summer for the next seven years.

Especially on those wonderful fall days in September and October, we were usually reluctant to make the return trip home too early and often delayed our departure until four or five o'clock, making it eight or nine before we would get home. The best part about the trip back was our usual stop at Gene-O's roadside restaurant for broasted chicken. We needed something substantial in our stomachs by then because of the limited fare in the cabin. On arriving home, we immediately unloaded the pickup and trailer, working quickly and without much comment to clean out the ice chests, store the water jugs, return tools I had used, slide dirty clothes down the laundry chute, and whatever else needed to be done. Neither one of us wanted to get up in the morning and see a mess. This only took 15 or 20 minutes, and soon after, Kathy and Kirby were off to bed and asleep. I could never shut down that quickly after the long drive and busy weekend, so I would sort through the mail and maybe check a few headlines in the papers. Then, in the quiet and semi-dark of the house, I would sit back in my recliner, trying to collect myself. More than once I asked myself, "What am I doing? Why am I doing all this?" But, then, I would look up at the living room wall above the sofa and see Kathy's painting. I didn't need to question anymore, for the answer was on the wall, and off to bed I would go, crawling in next to Kathy and drifting off to a peaceful sleep.

6

NEIGHBORS AND MEMORIES

When we talked about homesteading, Kathy and I agreed that we would try to be good neighbors wherever we would go and to participate in community life. We weren't seeking to hide or escape by living in the woods. We understood happiness would depend on the relationships we had with our neighbors down the lane and in the larger community. Some things we took care of right from the start. We decided we would buy from local merchants so that when we patronized their stores they would know us and greet us. We knew we could save money by buying lumber from the big retail outlets, but we chose to buy instead from the local hardware/lumber store in town. Following this practice, we got to know the grocery clerks, convenience store operators, café owners, bank tellers, and others who eventually would greet us by our first names. Likewise, we have never regretted hiring local carpenters, electricians, plumbers, and excavators. Joining a local church and becoming acquainted with its members, some of whom have become good friends, also helped make us feel at home.

We didn't have many "neighbors down the lane" to get to know. When we bought the land, our closest neighbors in any direction lived nearly a mile from us, and there were only five people actually living on our road. Two of the neighbors proved especially memorable. Our farmer friend, Fred, was the first local person I met, and he was the first person we turned to when we needed help. Chris, who sold us the land, told us we needed to get to know Fred, and we would eventually come to understand that everyone knew him and had probably stopped at his farm down by the lake. That's where you could find him leaning on his pickup or sitting on his parked four-wheeler visiting with someone who happened to come by. The township road snakes around the lake and then makes a sharp turn to the left at Fred's farmstead before heading straight west toward our place and beyond. Fred's old garage sits close to the road, and that is where callers would stop and park if they saw him working outside. He always had time to visit and stories to tell. A fairly big man, Fred had an easy laugh and manner and wanted to get to know newcomers. But his easy manner didn't keep him from speaking his mind, and if he didn't like something, he wasn't shy about hiding the fact. Some people may have taken offense at this, but most knew that was just Fred. An active member of the local American Legion post, the Lions Club, and his church, Fred could tell you a lot about the early settlement of the area and the life of its first settlers, which included his parents. He was a college graduate and didn't marry until his 50s. He and his wife, Willa, lived in separate homes on separate lakes. Willa was a widow when she married Fred, and the two of them thought it was best to continue maintaining their separate homes rather than establish one residence. No one thought much about this unusual situation, and both Fred and Willa seemed content with it.

For many years Fred milked cows, but later just kept some beef cattle and put up a little hay and maybe oats. Kathy said she once counted 13 different tractors on his place in various states of repair, although he used probably only three or four of them. His farm bordered a large recreational lake, and he sold off lots to several family members, who built cabins and homes there.

Fred was frugal and loved a bargain, attending local auctions whenever he could. He once bought a pickup load of new asphalt shingles of various colors and designs and didn't hesitate to put them on his barn and house even though the colors and styles didn't match.

In later years, I served with Fred on the township board, which he had been part of for 50 years in one capacity or another. He would pick me up to go look at a road, and as we drove around he would point out where loggers once drained a wetland, or where the old county road use to be, or where someone's property line runs. The other township supervisors and I weren't far off the mark when we kidded him that he knew the location of every township road culvert, and when they were put in. A few years before we moved to the area, friends started to call the road that runs past Fred's place "Freddie's Freeway" because the pavement ended just past his garage entrance. It was a money decision entirely, as the board could only afford to pave a portion of the road at the time, but it made for a good laugh. While I was on the board, the rest of the road was paved, including the stretch past Hiram Hill. These same folks then started calling it "Turgeon's Turnpike."

Several times when I was riding with Fred in his

caused high water problems. He placed a charge in the dam to blast out a hole so that the water level would be lowered behind the dam and along a road near there that ran between two lakes. When the charge went off, it blew a bigger hole than Fred anticipated, and the water began pouring through the gap into a wetland. The rushing water soon filled the center of the wetland, turning it into a small lake, and then continued its flow to a point where a small creek began. Down the creek the water roared before being funneled into a large, square concrete culvert beneath the driveway of a family that lived nearby. By then, Fred had run back through the woods to his pickup and drove over to the road, concerned that the water might take out the culvert. The little creek was now a river, and the water rushed through the culvert and rose to the level of the road. Fred thought for sure the culvert would surrender to the force of the water, but, fortunately, it didn't. Soon, the level dropped, and the danger was over. He blew holes in that dam after that, but used a lesser charge, and though the water level always rose in that culvert when the beaver dam was dynamited, it never again threatened to take it out. When I needed to deal with a high water problem along that road, I would make holes in the dam by removing the sticks and logs by hand, one piece at a time, to assure that I wouldn't make too large of a gap, ever mindful of the consequences of Fred's big blast.

There are other stories about Fred and dynamite, as well. Fred asked John, a mutual friend of ours, to take down some oak trees that were shading his hay field and keeping the grass from growing. John is a woodworker and jumped at the chance to get the oak, asking me if I would help him with the job. One of the oaks sat in the middle of the field, and when it came time to cut it down, we hooked a long chain to its trunk and connected the chain to a come-along attached to John's truck. John was to cut the tree, while I tightened the chain to make sure it fell where intended. While he was attaching the come-along, I stood by the tree and suddenly noticed a stick of dynamite at its base. I hollered at John, and we immediately went over to Fred's house to tell him what we had discovered. "Oh, yeah," Fred said. "I was going to blast that tree, but it didn't go off. I planned to wait a couple of days and go back, but forgot all about it." John and I retrieved our chain and never did cut down the tree. It still stands there today.

Fred is one of those fellows whom people say you could write a book about. I could echo that sentiment, even though I knew him for only about a dozen years. Fred died in 2006, and the neighborhood sorely misses him.

Another remarkable resident of the neighborhood lived just west of Fred. Elaine became our friend soon after we bought the land, and it's likely we have never met anyone like her before or since. Chris told us about Elaine when we bought the land from him. He and Elaine became close friends, and Chris would return to visit her even after he left Minnesota. In 1979, following her husband's death, Elaine moved from Wichita, Kansas, to her family's old place next to Fred's farm. She gave her Wichita home to her sister and moved into a humble structure without water or electricity on her property. A master gardener with a college degree, she chose a simple life in the country, tending to chickens and a goat and working in her wonderful gardens. Elaine was deeply spiritual, maintained a daily journal in spiral notebooks that over the years filled boxes, and was sought out by many for counsel. Members of an Indian tribe used to visit her, staying most of the day. A young woman would come more than 30 miles just to see her. Elaine's home was hardly more than a tar paper shack for many years until her nephews found an old, but serviceable, former resort cabin that they moved in and hooked to a septic system and electric power. She rarely left her home, but used the telephone regularly as her connection to the world. Her niece would bring her groceries. Though religious, she never proselytized, at least not us. Rather, she loved to converse about gardening, the woods, animals, and what was going on in our lives.

She was concerned about the road into her place, and sometimes I would blade it for her, but it was mostly sand, and I couldn't do much with it. She put hay down in the road's holes in hopes the grass would eventually break up enough to help fill them. We think the road was a concern because she wanted to make sure it wouldn't prevent visitors from coming.

Elaine began to develop some health problems a few years after we moved to our property, and we tried to help her as much as we could, cutting grass, tending to her chickens, splitting firewood, helping her with garden work, and cleaning the cabin. I built her a wood box so she would have a good supply of dry firewood right in the house, and she was grateful. Later on, she had to move into a nursing home for a while, but returned again to her home. When she passed away, we knew someone special had graced our lives.

Good neighbors help each other out. Fred brought manure to Elaine for her gardens and gave us a trailer load for ours. In turn, I helped him load hay bales and put them in his barn. Fred loaned me his big trailer to haul my tractor to the repair shop, and I helped him cut firewood for his stove. I plowed gardens for several neighbors using a plow Fred let me borrow, and those same neighbors helped Fred chase down his cows when they "went on vacation." This kind of thing goes on throughout the countryside, and it enriches and nurtures our lives. Thank God for good neighbors.

7

PLANTING TREES, DIGGING ROCKS

After the shop/cabin shell went up in June of 1994, we welcomed a steady stream of visitors, which cut into our time for getting work done, but gave us a lot of enjoyment nonetheless. We put off the task of insulating the walls and ceiling until October and instead concentrated on jobs like painting the storage shed, putting in railroad ties for tire stops in front of the cabin, and, as always, cutting brush along the edges of the meadows.

We are determined to keep our meadows as large as possible. I wouldn't like to live in a place encompassed by trees, and Kathy, Kansas girl that she is, absolutely couldn't. She needs some open space around her, and Hiram Hill has just enough to make us both happy. The meadows are peaceful places for dogs to run, the wind to blow over the tall grass, and for the eye to behold the beauty of the woods in the background. Each meadow is connected by trails and narrow passages, so it is like entering a different room in a new house, never certain what you will encounter or what you will see. The meadows are places where I can stand quietly and observe the landscape, noting the many young birches growing up in a brushy area above a little wetland, or how the beaver have harvested large amounts of alder in the lowlands off the pond. Over there, I can see the remains of an old deer stand in a beautiful birch clump atop a knoll on the meadow's edge. As the dogs run freely with their noses to the ground, on my left I catch a glimpse of our house through a narrow gap in the trees, and on the right I see the neighbor's barn reflected in the big pond across the way. Every chance to walk through the meadows is a blessing, and I am convinced the dogs know it's special, too. Just say, "Let's go for a run," and they bark their approval and head for the trails, grateful, it seems, just to run free and spend time with their master.

While construction work always occupied our time, we also enlivened our days with things that interested us. I joined the Bluebird Recovery Project and built and placed 10 bluebird nest boxes around the property. Observing the arrival of bluebirds in the spring always gave us pleasure, and I carefully monitored each box to check on the number of eggs, how many hatched, and when the little birds took first flight, reporting all this to the recovery project.

Planting trees also occupied my time each spring. Our land did not have an abundance of pine and spruce when we bought it, so it would be up to me to change that. Each spring I bought 500 pine, spruce, balsam fir, and tamarack seedlings from the state nursery nearby and planted them by hand, using a planting fork borrowed from the local Department of Natural Resources office. Most years, I drove up to Hiram Hill alone, picked up the seedlings and did the planting. It was hard, but satisfying work walking around with a bucket of seedlings and the heavy fork in the middle of May looking for good spots to plant trees. Norway and jack pines need full sun, while white spruce and white pine tolerate some shade. Tamaracks need full sun, also. Plunging the fork in the ground and moving it back and forth a couple of times, I made a slot in the earth to slip in the seedling's roots. Then with another stab of the fork adjacent to the first, I pressed the earth up against the roots – and hoped rains would water the young tree to get it off to a good start. I planted 100 seedlings each session, then rested, and maybe planted another batch later in the day. Most years, I shared some of the seedlings with neighbors and also bought small numbers of different species to add to the mix. I kept a record each year of the seedlings planted:

Number and Species

1995

28 sugar maple

4 Norway maple

100 white spruce

100 white pine

200 Norway (red) pine

50 jack pine

1996

100 tamarack

200 white spruce

100 balsam fir

100 white pine

6 blue spruce

1997

50 Norway (red) pine

50 white cedar

90 balsam fir

100 white spruce

100 black spruce

44 Scots pine

7 black walnut

1998

200 Norway (red) pine

100 jack pine

200 black spruce

The seedlings became my babies, and they needed tending. As the seedlings grow, deer love to eat their tops, or leaders, particularly the pines. So, each fall I cut up six-inch squares of paper and walked from tree to tree folding a paper over each leader and stapling it. This kept the deer from biting off the top, and allowed the tree to grow straight. In early May, I would retrace my steps, carrying a bucket and plucking off the paper protectors, because by then the deer preferred green grass and deciduous shoots over pine leaders. Once the trees grew tall enough, the deer couldn't reach the leaders, and I no longer had to staple on the paper squares. Many of the seedlings perished because of dry conditions and deer browsing, but many survived. It is a pleasure today to see 20-foot-tall red pines flourishing on the edges of the meadows and to rediscover vigorous young tamaracks and black spruce in remote spots that

I had forgotten about altogether.

Cutting firewood also was a happy task for us and has remained so through the years. There always is a tree that needs to be removed or one that falls over and needs to be cut up. We installed the wood stove in the cabin in the summer of 1995, so having a supply of wood was a necessity. We also needed a place to stack the wood, and until our wood shed was a reality, we piled the wood on inexpensive, but handy, wood racks that I designed and built. The bottom of the rack is comprised of two eight-foot-long treated lawn timbers tied together by short pieces of two-by-fours. The ends are made of two four-foot-high lengths of rebar, which in turn are tied together at the top with two-by-fours. I stack the wood on the lawn timbers between the sets of rebar, running a light chain across the top to hold the ends together. The racks are easy to build, and I wrote an article about the design for *Country Journal* magazine. Kathy had the article matted and framed, and it now hangs in our mudroom.

We wrapped up the season in 1994 by installing the insulation in the cabin. A local mason had just finished putting in the chimney, and it was time to button up for the winter. The next year would emerge with a flurry of activity, but with another winter to build things in the basement, read homesteading books, and make plans, we felt we were ready for anything it would bring.

The well diggers put in our well on April 7, and soon after I was digging myself – a 40-foot trench to bury the electric line from the cabin's power box to the well. The well, with its pipes and pressure tank, sat un-protected on our hill, and I became concerned one early May evening when I heard it was going to freeze hard up north overnight. So I called Fred, and he placed a tarp over the well, and kept it there until I came up the next weekend with a small well house I made out of scraps gleaned from a fire pit near an industrial con-struction site. The workers threw sheathing and lumber in the pit to be burned, often with nails in it, but if you were Johnny-on-the-spot, they didn't mind you salvag-ing what you could. To prevent possible freeze damage, I insulated the well hut and would leave a light bulb on inside if cold weather were expected. Having water was a wonderful thing after having to haul up our own sup-ply in jugs the previous two years. I soon rigged up a hose from the well house to a picnic table sitting under a big red oak near the cabin. There, the hose fit into a makeshift stand with a spigot. I always called it "Kathy's water station," and made other water stations by the pig pens and chicken coop in the years ahead, supplied by hoses running several hundred feet from the house.

Kathy and I started putting up the oriented strand board sheathing on the walls and ceiling a week before the well went in. It was cold and dreary, and snow still covered the ground. We had a little ceramic heater to keep us warm, but it just didn't do the job, and by the day's end, tired from the hard work, we looked at each other and knew tonight we needed to check into the local motel for a hot shower and a good sleep. We permitted ourselves such luxuries from time to time without guilt over the extra expense. In the middle of the month, we returned to finish the job, coming back the next weekend to put primer on the walls and ceiling. In another month, the walls were painted, and I installed some home-made cabinets and a large work bench I had built, which would serve as our kitchen counter. We painted the floor, put down a large carpet remnant, set up a bed, and installed the wood stove and a sink that drained into a bucket. The two of us collaborated on a room divider – I built the frame, and Kathy sewed the curtain – to give us some privacy in our makeshift bedroom. We then moved in our kitchen table and chairs and the pine Adirondack furniture, bookcase, and storage chest. Presto! We finally had a finished cabin, and I think we surprised ourselves at how nice it looked.

About that same time, while traveling through a small town on our usual route up north, I saw a Ford 8N tractor for sale along the road and inquired about it. Larry, the affable retired Land O'Lakes creamery worker who lived there, took me to his workshop, where I was amazed to see about a dozen little Ford tractors of various models and years. He restored them as a hobby. My dad farmed with these small tractors, and I spent hundreds of hours on them as a youth, plowing, cultivating, hauling bales, and raking hay. They are easy to handle and maintain, and I wanted one to replace the tractor I had purchased the year before and sold the previous fall. I used that tractor – an International 300 utility model with a front-end loader – for moving dirt and sand around the construction site, but found it hard to steer and difficult to maneuver on the rough terrain of Hiram Hill. A little Ford would do much better, I thought, so I bought a 1951 model from Larry for $2,000, giving him an additional $150 for a blade to mount behind it for grading our road. He took my check and immediately loaded the tractor and blade on

and Kathy and I gamely took on this task in early August. It was to be a pole building with a gabled roof and grooved plywood siding. We were excited as we laid out the building dimensions on the rough ground just west of the shop/cabin, and our first job was to drill six holes for the five-by-six-inch posts we had to install. I rented a hand-held auger with a gasoline engine on top. Kathy grabbed the handles on one side, while I took hold of those on the other side. I then pulled the starter rope, and the engine roared. As we pushed the auger down onto the first spot we had marked, the machine jerked violently, sending Kathy flying. I held on, but fell over. We had hit a big rock just inches below the surface. That slowed us down considerably, as I spent the next half-hour digging out the rock with a shovel and pry bar. The rock still sits at that corner of the building as a reminder of our labor. That would not be the first encounter with a stubborn rock by any means. Anyone who digs holes in our neck of the woods finds rocks. They are everywhere and often surprise me in interesting ways.

When excavating for our house, the workers dug up numerous large rocks that they rolled to the side. When the house was built and a young fellow came back to level the ground, he asked me what I wanted to do with the rocks. I told him to make a pile at a spot just to the southeast of the house near a stand of birches and to roll the rest down the hill and into a brushy low area there. With his skid loader he pushed and lifted the rocks into place, and, when finished, looked for a thumb's up from me. I thought the pile looked good, but never inspected it closely until much later. After we had moved into the house, I stood in the living room and noticed that the largest boulder facing the house had the face of a man on it. Curving around the side and over the top of his head was the long torso and face of a little dachshund, as if the dog were resting there. "Kathy, you've got to see this," I yelled. "Take a look at that rock. That's me and Kirby."

The rock pile is an important place on our homestead. Kathy later made it into a flower bed as well, and we planted bittersweet, which now covers much of the pile. We installed a flagpole and homemade sundial there and also a Kansas post rock with our name on it. In some parts of Kansas they once used limestone rock for fence posts, and people now salvage them and have their names carved on the sides for display. One of my brothers picked up a flat piece of rock on a farm in Quebec that our family's ancestors owned 350 years ago, and that rock sits on the boulder with the faces.

One spring day after we moved north, I decided to dig up the many rocks in our yard that I invariably hit with the lawn mower blade. When Kathy came home that afternoon, she said the place looked like the surface of the moon. Black holes where rocks once rested marred the surface in every direction. After digging around the rocks and using my pry bar to lift them, I many times had to wrap a log chain around them and pull them out with the tractor. Then I rolled the rocks onto the carryall on the back of the tractor and hauled them to a pile on the edge of the woods. Even though you think you have removed all the rocks, in future springs you will discover that new ones have surfaced, lurking there like half-submerged crocodiles, ready to strike the lawnmower.

Rocks also have surprises, if you are unlucky. When building the network of trails around the property, we not only had to cut brush and some trees, but also had to take out roots and rocks in the way so that we could disk and seed the paths to grass. Down the trails Kathy and I would go, stopping the tractor to dig out another rock or pull it out with a chain, if necessary. One big rock proved quite stubborn near the end of the day, so I dug deeper and pried it up with my bar. In the process, I disturbed a nest of yellow jackets and ended up getting stung. The rock hasn't been moved from the spot where I rolled it with my pry bar, and it will probably stay there for a long time.

People who have lake cabins generally like rocks and often ask landowners if they have any to give them to use on their lakeshore or for landscaping. According to Fred, my farmer friend, giving rocks away was OK with him for a while, but then he began to think that it was his hard labor that produced the rock pile, and, by golly, maybe these people ought to pay a little for his rocks. Excavators charge cabin owners for rocks, so why not landowners? I don't know whether Fred ever charged anyone, but I do know that he was impressed when, John, our mutual friend, first moved to the area and asked Fred if he could pick rock in his fields. Fred gave him permission, and that was the start of a long friendship. The term, "picking rock," completely baffled Kathy when she first heard it, but I assured her that in many places the activity is essential if farmers are going to protect their expensive equipment from damage when they work their fields. When my chance came to play farmer, I struck a deal. A fellow from a nearby lake asked me if I had any rocks. I knew he had a skid loader and large trailer, so I told him I had some rocks for him piled up, but also needed some rocks dug out in the yard around my barn. He was happy to oblige and dug out many rocks for me, which he happily hauled away for his lake place.

Gardens not only produce vegetables, but also rocks – lots of them. Every spring new ones rise to the surface. Fortunately, as time passes, they get fewer and smaller. My friend, Ferris, has a fine tiller mounted behind his John Deere garden tractor and comes by each spring to till our gardens. I am always worried that our latest crop of rocks will damage the tiller, but it hasn't happened. Ferris takes a load of rocks home with him to his lake place every now and then, so we all come out winners.

The wood shed project kept us busy for several weekends, but by late September we had it built and painted with a modest pile of wood stacked in one of the stalls. The second stall provided me with a place to store my tractor for the winter. We were a little upset in August when, after arriving one weekend, we discovered that someone had broken into the cabin and taken a camera, cassette player, flashlight, and a couple of walking sticks I had made, but nothing else. No tools were missing from the storage shed. We didn't feel good about it, but still had a good stay, taking time off to canoe the Crow Wing River with my son, Matt, and his wife, Jeni, who were visiting us from Missouri.

It was nice to come up in September and October and start a fire in our Wonderwood circulator. The $25 stove kept life cozy for us those cool autumn days, as we went about buttoning up for winter and feeling pretty good about everything, in spite of the break-in. We were in the cabin, we had water and electricity, and we had built a woodshed. Now, we could look ahead to 1996 and get serious about our plans for building a house on Hiram Hill.

8

Trails, Porcupines, and Decisions

B ig things were happening across the pond when we returned to Hiram Hill in the spring of 1996. We had new neighbors. A young couple purchased the remaining 57 acres of the 100-acre farm Chris had bought a number of years earlier. The couple and their three children had already moved to their new place, even though there was no house on the property. They temporarily camped out in the loft of the little llama barn, cooking their meals below as they began the major task of converting the main barn next to the pond into a home. They soon created livable space in the barn and then continued to work on it after moving in. They converted the barn's big loft into their main living quarters and also built bedrooms in a second loft. We were happy to have new neighbors and to hear the sounds of hammers and saws – as well as the shouts and laughter of children – coming from across the pond.

We made 23 trips to Hiram Hill that spring, summer and fall, and it became a critical time for us, as we debated whether to make Hiram Hill our permanent home or put off any such move indefinitely. Life there had pretty much taken on a slower pace. We had a nice cabin to stay in, and we enjoyed our weekends, watching finches, orioles, and hummingbirds at our feeders and observing the activities of the tree swallows and bluebirds at the nesting boxes. I enjoyed sitting in front of the cabin in the warm morning sun and listening to the snipe high above circle and swoop down in its mating ritual, making the "woo-woo-woo" sound that thrills me when I first hear it in the spring. To me, the snipe, more than the robin, means spring has returned. It loves this land of slough, pond, woods, and meadows and circles above for hours at a time.

Kathy and I discovered that beavers had taken down a half-dozen poplars up on Beaver Point, so we put on our gloves and went to work cutting up the trees for firewood and dragging the remaining branches to a burning pile in the middle of the adjoining little meadow. While we were at it, we cut down some of the brush among the trees on the hill, and I later planted some white pine and spruce seedlings there. Along the edge of the woods to the west of the main hill, we planted a dozen two-foot-high balsam firs that I had ordered from a Wisconsin nursery, and Kathy now can look at these beautiful trees through the kitchen window. We took walks down the township road, and it was always a pleasure when someone stopped to visit and fill us in on news from the neighborhood.

But we had one big job ahead of us, and we knew it must be completed if we were going to enjoy our land to the fullest. That job was to build a network of trails crisscrossing our woods and meadows. Trails open up the land for walking and observing nature, for hunting and reaching remote spots, and for gathering chokecherries, wild plums, cranberries and, of course, firewood.

In early June on our way north we stopped in a town and bought a rotary brush hog to mount on the back of the Ford tractor. With a front-end loader, the implement dealer loaded the brush cutter in the trusty Apache. After arriving at Hiram Hill, I asked Fred to use his tractor to lift the heavy implement out of the trailer. Before long, I had the brush cutter mounted on the Ford and ready to go. We had a good idea of where the trails should be cut, and the plan was to go in a general direction, stay on high ground, and avoid trees. In many places, the brush was dense, and it was difficult to see ahead. Kathy followed behind me on foot as I steered the tractor over the brush, pushing it down so the cutter's thick steel blades could whack it to pieces. The tractor would lunge forward, crashing into the thick brush. I had to stand up to see over the under-growth and steer clear of any trees. My straw hat flew off several times, and Kathy said I looked like someone riding a rodeo bull. But we pushed on, starting at our west meadow and running south along a ridge of oak trees leading to the edge of our property. The ridge bor-ders a long, narrow wetland that curves to the east and connects with a large wetland and pond to the south on county property. We cleared another trail on the other side of this narrow slough running back north to the homestead, as well as several other shorter, intercon-necting trails. The trails, about five-feet wide, bend and twist over the rolling terrain, making for a more inter-esting walk than along a straight line. Once the trails were cut in, the hard work began. We walked each trail with loppers in our hands to clip off all the brush stubs that protruded into the pathway and cut away the over-hanging tree and bush branches. We picked up all the debris and stacked it in piles along the way, coming back later to haul all this to our burn pile. Then, we removed the numerous rocks that protruded in the path, digging them out with a shovel and pry bar and using the tractor to pull them out when necessary. It was a lot of work, but the reward was instant: We loved being able to walk our land to see it close up.

We spent a couple of weekends making the trails, and then on another trip we stopped again and bought a five-foot tandem disk so I could smooth out the paths and prepare them for seeding. I passed over the trails five or six times with the disk, working up the ground as best I could. I then seeded it to mostly clover, which deer and ruffed grouse came to appreciate. Fred had given me a section of an old drag, and I pulled this over the seeded ground, giving the pathway a fairly smooth surface. The grass and clover seed took immediately, and we soon had a carpet of green along the curving, undulating trails. We knew we had done something right when the neighbor boy came over and rode the trails on his mountain bike, followed by his dog, Bree.

The two machinery purchases – the brush hog and disk – proved their worth in making the trails, but also continue to help me with other jobs. I use the brush hog each fall to knock down alder and hazel brush, as well as raspberry canes and weeds, in our meadows. Neighbors call on me to disk their garden plots when they become overgrown. If I plow new space for them, the disk effectively cuts up the plowed soil for more efficient tilling later. At about $500 each, the two implements were big purchases for us at the time, but worth every penny on a homestead like ours.

A burglar took some of the fun out of our Fourth of July weekend, when we discovered that about $900 worth of tools and other items had been taken from the cabin and our storage shed. Among the missing items were a lawn mower, ladder, and wheelbarrow. Fortunately, the burglar, who later was arrested, didn't damage any property, using a bolt cutter to cut the padlocks on the gate and storage shed. He gained entry to the cabin by pushing open the door latch with a putty knife or other thin blade. But we didn't let it trouble us too much and went on with our plans. Amanda and my sister, Alyce, came that weekend, and we rode bicycles on the paved state biking trail and canoed in the Shell and Crow Wing rivers during the gorgeous, sunny few days.

On Memorial Day weekend, a porcupine visited us, and I noticed him gnawing on the plywood gussets nailed to the rafters in our wood shed. Porcupines like the taste of something in the glue in plywood, and we would have numerous encounters with them as we defended our buildings from their assaults. On this occasion, in broad daylight, the porcupine continued his lunch while I tried to scare him away. Nothing seemed to work, and Kathy said we should shoot him. That was just fine with me, except I didn't have a rifle. We put in a call to Fred, but he wasn't home, so we called his relative who lived on the lake next to him. In minutes, a man we hadn't met before came over with his son and another relative and told us to chase the porcupine out of the wood shed so he could dispatch him. After a lot of commotion and yelling, the animal climbed down the wood pile in the shed and scurried out the front and around the side. The man shot him as he was going into the woods. Kathy and I figured this would take care of the problem, but the very next weekend, another porcupine paid us a nocturnal visit in the shed, chewing on the gussets like the first porcupine. I heard the unmistakable sound at 11 p.m. while in bed. This time, I managed to scare off the critter without much trouble and went back to sleep. With no further porcupine visits that we were aware of, we forgot about the problem until I was awakened at midnight late in July as we slept with the doors and windows open to stay cool. Another porcupine was out there. I ran out to the shed wearing only my underwear and carrying a flashlight. Having no success yelling, pounding on the wall, or throwing pieces of firewood at the critter in the rafters, I decided to get the GMC and drive it up to the shed in hopes the noise and glare of the headlights would make a difference. With the truck in place, its engine running, and head-lights on high, I threw some more firewood at him and even honked the pickup's horn, but it was to no avail. Finally, I grabbed a stick to poke him. Unbeknownst to me, Kathy had crept close behind me holding a metal cooking pot and a large ladle, and just as I was ready to jab the creature, she started to bang the pot loudly with the ladle. I jumped and yelled, "What the heck are you doing? You scared me!" She said she was just trying to help, and as we looked at each other and considered the improbable scene, we both had to laugh before get-ting back to the business at hand. I finally did poke the porcupine, and frightened, it went down the back of the shed and into the woods. Then, as I was picking up the pieces of firewood and tossing them back onto the pile, I felt some painful pricks on my bare legs. In the dark I couldn't tell what had happened. I figured some loose porcupine quills on the firewood must have somehow pricked me, and let it go at that.

Unfortunately, our porcupine encounters weren't over. After we had moved to Hiram Hill, I built a chicken coop and also sided it with grooved plywood siding. Before I was even finished with it, a porcupine came at night to gnaw on the newly-installed siding. You could see his chew marks about 12 to 15 inches off the ground all around the building. I had to put tar paper around the lower third of the structure as protection until I could paint it. You can still see his many teeth marks showing today. After we built our barn, a porcupine paid us several nighttime visits, chewing away at our siding and damaging one of our big sliding doors so badly that I had to take it off and replace part of a panel. Try as I might, I could never catch the porcupine at work, even when I parked my pickup next to the barn and waited there with my rifle in the dark.

Yes, I finally owned a rifle and didn't have to call on the neighbors, but that didn't proceed smoothly, either. My sister, Alyce, gave me the 30-30 rifle, reminding me that it once belonged to my dad. One evening, shortly after I finished building the chicken coop, our dog,

Cooper, looked out our low bay window and spotted a porcupine crawling across the lawn. He began barking loudly. Kathy looked out, figuring it was just another deer, but then yelled out, "Bill, it's a porcupine! Get your rifle. It must be the one that's eating the chicken coop." By then, the porcupine had climbed up a tree, and we could see him plainly, sitting on a limb about 25 feet off the ground.

Reaching in the closet, I grabbed the rifle, still in its case, and took it out. I thought I had a few bullets in my dresser, but to my chagrin I could only find one. "You've got to be kidding," Kathy said. "One bullet? How come you didn't get some bullets to use?" I really didn't have an explanation, but told her I could get it with just one shot, as if I knew what I were talking about. I went outside, walked to the tree, took aim, and fired. To my great surprise, the porcupine jumped and then fell to the ground dead. "Wow, good job, honey!" my proud spouse said. "Nothing to it," I replied. Now, I really don't have a grudge against porcupines and don't seek them out to do harm, but they need to stay in the woods and do their chewing there, not in my yard.

In early August, Kathy's parents and her sister and family came to visit. After driving up from home, we

of welding cylinders, with a loop and horizontal bar at the top for hanging and for ornamentation. I liked them and thought it would be nice to have one on Hiram Hill so Kathy could call me by ringing the bell if I were out in the woods. The folks at the welding shop were reluctant to part with any of their old cylinders. They feared someone might try to put one back in service even though they are condemned and for safety reasons are not to be used again. I had no such intentions, of course, and explained to them what I wanted to do, but to no avail. As I was leaving, a worker there told me he had several old, empty cylinders at his home and would give me one. He pointed to some bushes near the welding supply store and said he would put one there, and that I could pick it up the next time through. I gave him $5 for his trouble and hoped he would do as he promised. Returning home on Sunday, I checked the bushes and was pleased to find my cylinder. I quickly loaded it in the back of the pickup and went on my way. Later, I took it to a welding shop and described what I wanted, following my own design. A week later the shop had my bell finished, except for a clapper. I fashioned one out of a hardwood ball that I had found at a craft shop. I hung the ball inside, added a rope to grab when ringing the bell, and painted the outside black. The bell has an excellent sound and can be heard throughout our property. Once the house was built, I hung it on our porch.

During the summer, we carefully staked out where the house we were planning to build would be situated on our hill. This was exciting stuff for us, and we adjusted the stakes from time to time until we felt we had it right. The previous winter we had found a home plan we liked and asked the local lumber yard to give us an estimate. The estimator figured the house would cost about $100,000 when everything was included, and this was too much for us. Our existing home was paid for, and we figured we could get only $80,000 if we sold it. We were determined that the new house would not cost much beyond that amount, and we would not consider taking on a mortgage of any size. The home plan we found would have been a good fit with its open design and large windows to the south and east, but we had to come up with something different. Rather than buy another set of plans, I drew up my own plan, cutting down the square footage by 20 percent. Kathy liked my plan even more than the original because she would be able to see who would drive up when she was in the kitchen. So, we knew what was possible for us if we leave our jobs and pursue our homesteading dream on Hiram Hill. In January, I was to inform the college of my intentions to take early retirement, and Kathy, later in the spring, was to let her school know officially that she would not return the following year.

It was kind of scary – and awfully exciting.

9

A New House, a New Life

We had rolled the dice, and we were ready to deal with the realities ahead. Our biggest concern was health insurance. Fortunately, the state provided me one year of free insurance as part of an early retirement incentive, so Kathy and I would have coverage over the next 12 months under our existing plan. After that, we planned to buy individual catastrophic insurance policies with $5,000 or $10,000 deductibles. At the time, it seemed like the best alternative. We decided we would set aside enough money in a certificate of deposit at the bank to cover the deductibles should either of us get hurt or become seriously ill. We had some breathing room, but working out permanent health insurance coverage remained a priority.

Having enough money to live on was a bigger concern. We had a small savings account, and my early retirement incentive also included a modest severance award that would be paid out over three years. We determined that the severance pay would go directly into savings and was not to be used for living expenses. It would provide a cushion if we had to pull back from our plans at Hiram Hill and do something else. The hard reality facing us was this: Our income would drop to $480 per month, the sum of my state retirement check. That's only $5,760 per year. At 55 years old, I couldn't tap into my two annuities and IRA until turning 59 1/2 without incurring penalties. Social security would come later at age 62. We figured interest on our savings would total another $2,600 or so, and that would bring our income to a little over $8,300. Carefully estimating our expenses based on our experience where we were living, we thought we needed $15,000 to live on, meaning we had to earn about $6,700 more or $3,350 each. The best employment bet for Kathy was substitute teaching, which paid $80 per day. I would have to come up with some kind of job. In 1996, a year before we moved north, I had enrolled in a week-long class at the University of Minnesota on tax assessing, figuring I could possibly find some work as a contract township assessor.

I wasn't in a hurry to find a job because my real

work, particularly that first summer and fall in 1997, was to finish construction on our house. As we went along, we figured that everything I could do myself, such as building the kitchen cabinets, bathroom vanities, and bookcases, would save us more than my earning a few dollars at a minimum-wage job. That would prove true again, when I added a bathroom and several other rooms in our basement and built our chicken coop and barn.

We were convinced the $15,000 annual income would provide us with a comfortable standard of living. We didn't have a mortgage or car payment, and because we would heat our home with wood, there would be no heating bills. A friend gave me an old television antenna on a pole to mount against the house, and that meant we could get five channels over the air free of charge, saving us the possible expense of satellite TV. Basic Bill was on a roll. Our plan was to grow as much food as we could in our gardens, to butcher a couple of pigs each year, and tend to a flock of chickens for eggs and meat. Truthfully, the expenses to raise pigs and chickens generally exceed what it would cost to buy the meat and eggs at the store, but we always took satisfaction in having our own, organically-produced source of these foods.

Deep down, I welcomed the challenge of trying to live on $15,000. Finding ways to cut costs and to make something with my own hands instead of buying it somehow appealed to me. Kathy said the notion is empowering. Her frontier instincts drive her to use what's she given and make something of it. This attitude makes a person dig deep into his storehouse of creativity to discover the fullness of possibility. Cynics will criticize us and say that we never risked all that much, since we have our college degrees and plenty of opportunities to fall back on. All that is true. We didn't risk everything, but we did risk *something* by trying to rely on our own initiative and wits, at least to a degree. In the end, homesteading for us is a step in faith, a hope for the best, and a way to renew the spirit.

Others might say that the things we set out to do are ordinary. Many other country dwellers routinely accomplish these tasks and don't make a big deal about it. Again, that is all true. Except that, for me more than Kathy, homesteading became a way to help overcome doubts and build self-confidence. My life lacked passion, and I didn't know how to fix it. Sometimes while driving my pickup, I would listen to George Jones sing *Someday My Day Will Come* on the tape player. I had no clue how to make my "dreams become reality" as the lyrics suggest. I didn't know what my dreams were. Yet, slowly, Kathy's simple painting opened a door to understanding. It suggested to me that the plain and the ordinary things of rural life are necessary for balance and health, at least in my life. It shouldn't have been such a mystery. I have a couple of friends, now retired, who worked in data processing and statistical analysis in their professional lives. Both lived in the country, and as hobbies, one raised cattle and the other pheasants and deer. Both these men balanced the modern and technical aspects of their lives with the rural and mundane. They needed to be in touch with living things and get their hands dirty. I always admired them, but only later came to realize I needed that kind of balance in my life, too. So, if balance is what this is all about, so be it. Call it a personal journey. Whatever it is, it's real and life changing.

In February 1981, Kathy and I were married, and after a brief honeymoon, we lived apart for several months. I was in Minnesota, and Kathy remained in Kansas, finishing out the school year. Then, on June 1, Kathy sold her house, and we loaded a U-Haul truck with her belongings and moved to southwestern Minnesota, where I had been working for a couple of years. My job there, funded by a grant, had ended the day before, and I had applied for an opening at the college in town. That's all we had going for us when we drove the U-Haul to Minnesota. We had never even lived together. More than once she's asked me, "What was I thinking – marrying you, giving up my job, selling my house and moving away from my family, with neither one of us certain of getting a job?"

Once we got to Minnesota, I drove Kathy to several small towns so she could drop off her résumé at the superintendent's office in hopes there might be a job opening. As it turned out, the first school she visited ended up hiring her, and she began a 16-year teaching career there that fall. I ended up with the job at the college, and we were, you might say, on our way.

If good fortune came our way back in 1981, it also awaited us when we moved to Hiram Hill in July 1997. There, Kathy began seeking substitute teaching jobs in area schools when the school year started in September. In early October, she spotted a newspaper ad for a half-time teaching job at a school 30 miles away and applied for it. She got the job, but, after only two weeks, the school offered her a full-time, sixth-grade teaching position. There were too many sixth graders in the existing class, and the administration decided to divide it. Suddenly, everything changed for us. Continued health insurance coverage would now be a possibility, and our income situation would improve almost immediately. We never expected such a turn of events, but we welcomed it, of course.

Kathy's new job meant that my role on the homestead changed, as well. We decided that I would tend to the home fires, figuratively and literally, while she would hold down a job. I did the housework and laundry, made her lunch in the morning to take to school, and had supper ready when she came home. I learned to be a decent cook and made all of our bread. In addition, I took care of outdoor chores, cutting wood, splitting it, tending to pigs and chickens, mowing grass, turning compost, building furniture – whatever was required to make our place work. Kathy worked hard as a teacher, and most evenings you could find her grading papers and preparing lesson plans at the kitchen table. This division of labor satisfied both of us because it assured us that we could continue this lifestyle indefinitely and improve our place as we went along. If Kathy could continue teaching full time for another four years until she could take early retirement at 55, we would be in great shape.

We didn't know all this, of course, when we drove through the big storm that July day to begin our new life on Hiram Hill. After we had informed our respective schools during the winter that we would be leaving, we led a hectic life keeping up our jobs, arranging for our new house to be built, finding a buyer for our existing house, and preparing for the move. We took a day off from our jobs on March 12 to meet our excavator, Jack, at Hiram Hill. The stakes marking the corners of our house barely stood out in the two feet of snow on the hill, but they were visible enough for Jack to start digging the basement. He pushed the snow away with his pickup's snow plow and began digging with his machine. We had hoped to have a walkout on the east side of the basement, but it soon became evident that wouldn't work on the gentle slope, so we gave up on it. We were disappointed, but glad that the work was under way so soon, and we headed home. By April 5, the basement was in and the house framed, roofed, and shingled. Work would continue at a rapid pace, and near the end of May we were thinking about painting the interior walls. We hired contractors to put up the shell, install the insulation, sheetrock, windows, and doors,

where most of the heat is lost through the flue. We burn only three to four cords of wood each year. The radiant heater burns cleanly, so there is no soot in the firebox, only white ash that is pushed down a hole into an ash pit in the basement. The heater is built on a concrete block foundation extending from the basement floor. The fire burns behind the closed glass doors, so there never is any smoke smell in the house.

Our masonry heater also features a smooth granite bench on the front just below the firebox. As the heat passes through a channel underneath the top, it heats the granite and provides a warm place for us to sit when we come in from the cold. The radiant heat generated by the unit warms all objects around it – everything it "sees," so to speak, rather than heating the air as conventional furnaces do. All objects in the room – walls, ceiling, furniture, lamps, books and so forth – warm to an ambient temperature. As a result, there is very little difference in the temperature of the air from the ceiling to the floor. In conventional heating systems, the air is usually much warmer at the ceiling than the floor since warm air rises. Without much movement of air in the room, there is less dust. In the previous house we lived in, I battled sinus problems almost continually during the winter when our gas-fired forced air furnace operated.

Masonry heaters have been called the "Cadillac" of heating systems because of their efficiency. Although the fire reaches temperatures around 1,700 degrees at the height of the burn, the heaters have been described as having "fire in a safe." Completely enclosed in heavy layers of firebrick, as well as the outer brick covering, the heaters are safe to operate. Because they burn so hot, there is very little creosote build-up in the chimney. The chance of a chimney fire is virtually nil. In the first 10 years of operation, I cleaned the chimney only twice, and both times there was little soot to remove. Air comes into the heater's firebox through an eight-inch pipe from the outside running below the floor. Thus, inside air is not used to support combustion. Because the heaters' fires burn so hot and cleanly, they pollute the atmosphere far less than wood burning units that need to be dampened down to slow combustion.

Masonry heaters can be custom built to fit almost any situation. Ideally, they should sit in the middle of an open area so that the radiant heat being emitted can warm the area around it. They are suited for an open floor plan, where kitchen, dining room, and living room adjoin one another without doors or walls separating them. Our heater also sits close to a hallway leading to two bedrooms and a bathroom. The master bedroom is located farthest from the heater, but we never have had to turn on the electric baseboard heater in the room in all the years we have lived there, even during the coldest days of a Minnesota winter. We have found that the temperature in the main living area of the house stays between 69-72 degrees at all times during the winter when we are firing the heater. The master bedroom, at the north end of the house, is a few degrees cooler than that, but we prefer it that way for sleeping. We have several large windows on the east and south sides of the house. During the winter when it is sunny, solar heat coming through the windows also heats the house. Many times, when it's sunny and the outside temperature is between 20-30 degrees above, we only need to start a fire once a day, rather than twice.

I first read about masonry heaters in *Mother Earth News*, and I was intrigued not only with their efficiency, but also with their beauty. The heaters originated in Russia and Finland and are often called "Finnish contra-flow heaters." The contra-flow term describes the action of the heat rising up, down and around through the internal passageways before passing out through the chimney. A person might think that the chimney's draw would be hindered because of the circuitous route, but that is not the case.

Finding a mason to build a masonry heater could prove difficult in many areas, but we were lucky to find Dick, a mason who lived in the area. He has one in his house. When we drove up to his place one day to discuss with him our interest in having a heater built, he invited us into his home. Coming through the door, the first thing we noticed was his beautiful heater, faced with a North Dakota brick called Prairie Common. When he asked us what kind of brick we were considering and what design we had in mind, Kathy simply said, "We'd like a heater just like yours."

We had to wait until August before Dick arrived with his helper, Jack, to start building the heater, but that was fine with us because we were busy working on the house. It took two weeks for Dick and Jack to complete their work, and it was a great feeling when I helped them lift a big piece of two-inch thick granite on top of the unit, the last major step. Dick whistled while he worked, and his cheery disposition made him good company. While working one day, he asked me if

I would like some hooks put in the side of the heater, and I said sure. He came back the next day with three old railroad spikes that his sons had found. He painted them black and installed them, and we now hang our walking sticks on the spikes.

Dick told us that in the winter he goes down to Central America and trains church volunteers from the U.S. to lay brick and blocks. The volunteers then build school buildings and churches for the people living there. When he was finished with our heater, he took his wife and two sons on a canoe trip down the Pine River to the Mississippi and then south from there.

The masonry heater includes a bake oven on the back side. We use it for baking bread and cooking pot roasts. By noon or one o'clock, the oven's interior temperature has dropped to 325 degrees, time to put in a roast and cook it all afternoon. By five o'clock the temperature has dropped to 200 degrees or so, and supper is ready.

There are several firms that offer kits for building masonry heaters. The kits include specially designed firebrick that goes together like a puzzle, creating all the necessary heat channels for the heater. They can be purchased to include a bake oven as well. After following the steps to put together the insides of the heater, the mason can finish the outside with any kind of brick or stone.

Our heater cost $6,900 to build in 1997, and we paid another $80 for some 12-inch granite tiles to place on the floor surrounding the heater. Dick, our mason, found granite remnants to use for the bench, mantel and top of the heater, and this provided us with an outstanding feature at an affordable cost. The granite tiles on the floor were seconds, but you would be hard pressed to discover any flaws in them. We never batted an eye over the cost because we knew that this heating system would outlast us. There are no moving parts except for the latches on the firebox and oven doors and a lever that allows you to control a damper that sits atop the handsome chimney Dick built.

Our masonry heater not only occupies the center of our home, it occupies a central place in our hearts. Each winter morning, I get up early, get the coffee pot going, and go into the attached garage to get some firewood. I carry it in the house with our tote made from the Apache's canvas tent – the very first thing Kathy and I ever made for our homestead. Carrying the wood through the kitchen and to the heater, I rest the bundle on the granite bench, open the firebox doors and stack the wood in a cross-hatch fashion. I roll up two pieces of newspaper to put on the firebox floor between two splits of wood. On top of that, I slip in some kindling, often pieces of scrap pine lumber or tree bark. It's now time to light the newspaper, close the doors and let the fire take hold. Soon it is roaring, and the coffee is ready. Kathy and our dog, Cooper, get up and join me in the living room. We sit in there in the light of that fire, drinking our coffee and discussing our plans for the day. These morning sessions are valued moments in our lives, and we never tire of the experience. Cooper sits there quietly, enjoying the warmth and the sounds of our voices. On days when Kathy and I are away in the winter and can't sit by the heater, we miss it.

10

ROADMAPS AND LISTS

During the 1980s, my wife and I accompanied her parents on annual summer camping trips. They would drive up from Kansas, and we would head for the North Shore of Lake Superior, Wisconsin's Door County, Michigan's Upper Peninsula, or the Provincial Parks of Ontario. Her father had a tent camper for a while and then bought a hard-shell camper that we pulled behind his car. I did the driving, and we enjoyed our trips immensely, coming away with memories that we treasure today. But if you asked Kathy or me what year we went to Door County or when we rode the ferry to Mackinac Island, we would be hard pressed to come up with an accurate answer. It's likely we would take a guess and hope we were right. It would have been quite easy to make a note somewhere, marking the date and year that we made each trip. But we didn't, and unless we do a lot of searching around and deductive thinking, we probably will always do some guessing when we reminisce about these trips.

We didn't do any better when we began making those trips to central and northern Minnesota in search of land. Instead of writing down when and where we went, we unwisely left it all to memory. It's not hard to remember the details of the places we visited, and the experiences we had, but the timeline isn't clear in all cases. So, we are left to figure out the sequence of events and usually are frustrated when we can't.

So, after we bought our property, I decided to keep a record of each trip we made, what we did, the names of the people we talked to, and any other significant details. My entries, all written on a yellow legal pad, are brief and to the point. Reading them triggers the memory and puts me back in the moment. I also was determined to keep track of all our expenses, and I did that faithfully from start to finish every time we undertook a new, major project. So, it's not hard for me to know what our investment in Hiram Hill totaled at the end of 1997, six months after we moved there permanently:

TOTAL COSTS 1993-1997

House $87,807.86

Shop	10,196.41
Wood shed	1,114.74
Storage shed (trade)	1,100.00
Subtotal	100,219.01
Land, Well, Road, Other	22,403.55
Travel Expenses	2,889.84
Grand Total	$125,512.40

Both Kathy and I had good jobs during that period, and we put most of the excess dollars we earned into Hiram Hill. Kathy said several times that we probably would never recover our investment if we decided to sell the property some day, and I thought she had it right. To our surprise, demand for lakeshore in our area grew dramatically in the 1990s and skyrocketed in the years following. Real estate agents were busy people, and they used the expression, "They're not making any more lakeshore," to impress on their clients that there is only so much lake property available. As long as the demand for it increased, prices would rise, too. The soaring lake property market also increased the value of off-lake property, so we soon discovered that our land and homestead were worth more than we had invested. The price escalation started a year or two after we purchased our land. If we had waited even a few years longer, we could not have afforded to buy the property. It's likely we would have ended up with a five- or 10-acre parcel, rather than the 43 acres we bought. But, even small acreages are expensive now. No doubt, we acted at the right time.

By the end of 1997, we had four buildings on our place, but we were not finished with our plans for development of the property. The plan I had sketched out in 1993 was pretty much completed now, and we looked ahead and dreamed some more. As money became available, we were of like mind to pour it into further development, forgoing anything else, including vacations and travel. Our chief luxury was going out to breakfast after church or to the American Legion for a drink and meal with friends on Friday nights. We usually made one trip to Kansas to visit relatives, but that was about it. Trips to the Twin Cities occurred only if absolutely necessary. When I needed a tool to get a job done on Hiram Hill, I didn't hesitate to buy it. If it were going to be a major outlay, such as a riding mower or band saw, I would ask Kathy about it, but I knew the answer: We need it, so go ahead.

As we looked to the future, we knew we wanted to put a bathroom and a couple of bedrooms in the basement. We needed the room to accommodate family and friends who came to visit, and it was understood that I would work on those projects as money and time became available. A chicken coop was a priority, and a barn and pond, hopefully, would be realities within a few years. Our income would improve once I could begin to tap into my annuities and IRA at age 59 1/2, but that wasn't going to happen until 2002. I began to develop a general plan listing our goals and revised it whenever necessary. It looked like this:

Hiram Hill Plan

1998

Construct basement office/bedroom

1999

Build chicken coop

2000

Build wood shed addition

2001

Construct basement bathroom

Construct basement bedroom

Dig pond

2002

Build barn

We had a roadmap to follow – and a lot of work

to do in the years ahead. All along, I had a general idea of how I wanted the homestead to develop, particularly how the buildings should be situated for their best use. I knew as I grew older I probably would want to save as many footsteps between buildings as I could, but countered that in my head by saying walking is good and helps keep us healthy. That debate took place several times before we decided to put the wood shed where we did – about 75 feet west of the shop and about 200 feet from the house. Many homesteaders would question the wisdom of that. The shed sits where it is because I wanted to face it east and have an open grassy area in front for unloading logs and for cutting and splitting firewood. The eastern exposure and open, grassy area assures plenty of morning and afternoon sun, which helps dry wood stored inside and also is a relatively warm place to split wood in winter. Granted, it is a hot place to work in summer, but I don't split wood then. Further, I located the shed near the shop so I could put a floodlight on the latter building to light up the area at night. On several occasions, I forgot to fill the wood box at the house and had to put on my boots in the early morning to fetch an armload of wood. When that happens, I flip on the floodlight switch in the shop as I

them to town to be filled. I also have an 80-gallon gas tank and hand pump on a stand next to the shed for filling the tractor. We keep our push lawnmower, snow blower, shovels, pry bars, post driver, and other tools in the shed, as well as potting soil, lime, flower pots and the like. Since gasoline is stored there, I wanted the building to be a good distance from any of the others.

Even the placement of the chicken coop required thought. I located it fairly close to the shop and house because we needed to make frequent trips to the coop every day, especially when raising baby chicks under heat lamps. Our being able to run a garden hose to the coop for water was a must, also. I stored chicken feed in the southwest corner of the shop by a door that leads out directly to where the coop is located. Lastly, since the coop is situated up against the woods on two sides, I fenced in an area amid trees and brush to provide some shade and to hide the chickens' presence from hawks and eagles flying above.

We originally talked of locating our barn about 150 feet south of the house in the small meadow containing the "Three Sisters" ironwood trees, but that would have been a poor choice. There is no easy access for vehicles for one thing. We needed to locate our barn in a place near our pigs so we could store their feed in it, and I also wanted the barn to be near an apple orchard I hoped to develop. My dream is to have friends over each fall to harvest apples and press apple cider and serve them chili and crackers in the barn.

The terrain dictates a lot when it comes to situating buildings on a homestead, and you have to do what's possible or spend money moving trees and dirt to get what you want. We didn't do the latter; rather, we took what the uneven terrain gave us and came up with a reasonable layout. Level ground is hard to find on Hiram Hill. Kathy tells our friends that I dream of being able to mow a large, flat lawn somewhere with no rocks or bumps. What a luxury that would be.

When we bought the land, we didn't have it surveyed. In retrospect, it would have been wise to do so, but fortunately the decision did not come back to haunt us. It wasn't until 2005 that I lined up a surveyor and got the job done. It's costly to hire a surveyor, but when the job is finished, you know exactly where your property lines are. Once the surveyor showed me the location of the marking pins, I drove in steel fence posts to mark them on each corner of the property. In one place I couldn't pound a post in the ground because there was a rock directly below the pin, so I marked the spot with another big, flat rock and scratched an "X" on it. Once I marked each corner, I drew a map of the property in a notebook and indicated the location of each pin and post.

The notebook, which I keep in my desk, contains a lot more information than just the location of survey pins. In it, I also have noted the feed costs for my pigs and chickens; the dates we started seeds each year; the dates we planted our crabapple and apple trees and their locations; the dates the ice went out on our pond and a nearby lake, and the dates when major weather events occurred.

Honestly, I am not a record fanatic. Most of my notations are brief and, hopefully, are useful. In the future, I would like to open a new notebook on January 1, recording the temperature at, say, 6 a.m., the general weather conditions, and noting a few phenological observations during the day. The idea would be to do this *every single day* throughout the year. That would mean no overnight travel away from the homestead. Even so, doing such a thing somehow appeals to me. To observe and record the pulse of the seasons in one small spot on earth over the full course of a year seems a worthy endeavor. Perhaps there would be an article or another book in it. Or, perhaps it would just satisfy a soul in search of a simple and orderly journey through life.

Notebooks aren't the only thing I use to keep myself on track. I also make to-do lists for each season and find them indispensable in getting all the homestead tasks completed. Each year, I return to the list from the previous year to help me remember what I need to do. Then, I start the new list for that particular season. Looking back over these lists reminds me of how a homestead is never boring; there's always something to do, even in winter. There were 75 items on the spring 2000 list of things to do and 40 items on the fall 2000 list. Below are samplings from both lists:

SPRING 2000

1. Order seeds, plants
2. Set up pig pen
3. Expand chicken run
4. Build honeysuckle trellis
5. Remove straw from septic
6. Start seeds
7. Put manure on garden
8. Do taxes
9. Repaint trim on shop

10. Remove leaves from flower beds

11. Replace chicken litter

12. Pull off pine bud caps

13. Set out hoses to pigs, chickens

14. Service snow blower, store

15. Till garden

16. Take out ashes

17. Set up rain barrel

18. Get straw for pigs

FALL 2000

1. Dig potatoes, store

2. Bag and sort onions, store

3. Pick cranberries

4. Have hogs butchered

5. Take down pig pen

6. Prune raspberries

7. Clean small shed

8. Turn compost

9. Wash house windows

10. Put bud caps on pines

11. Empty rain barrel

12. Change oil in tractor

13. Cut brush in meadows

14. Clean chicken coop

15. Clean out bluebird boxes

16. Build set of sawhorses

17. Cut, split wood

18. Clean out shop gutter

It's a good feeling to complete a task and scratch off the item on the list. Kathy and I take that a step further in the interest of getting all the credit due. When we complete a job that isn't on the list, we make sure we add it and then happily scratch through it. Lists help me organize my time and set me on a course to accomplish something each day. Without lists, I would forget to do some things and get behind on my work. I've always told Kathy that even if we accomplish just one thing each day, we can call it progress. Of course, we usually accomplish more than that, but the thought motivates me. That doesn't mean I don't take time to take a break or just loaf. Quite the contrary. My favorite time for a break is in the afternoon on a sunny day in the fall, when I pour a cup of coffee and sit on our deck overlooking the pond across the way. I look at the fall colors on display and the peaceful scene surrounding me. I know it's a privilege to be there on the homestead in the middle of the day, taking a break from my simple, but worthy tasks. Of course, I always reach for the cookies in my shirt pocket, and the dogs, in turn, line up with tails wagging for their biscuits.

Barn begins to take shape, June 2002.

Kathy, Tara, Buddy, and view of pond and barn,
September 2002.

Kathy and Bill, September 2002.

Bill in front of red pines he planted, October 2006.

Bill chopping wood.

Tara and Buddy, 2007.

Winter on Hiram Hill, January 2004.

Our masonry heater.

11

MAKING WHAT'S NEEDED

Sometimes you have to look for tools in unlikely places. I drove up to the scrap yard hoping I might come away with a foot-long piece of old railroad track. I needed an anvil for my shop, and a section of steel track would serve the purpose. On the anvil, I can use a hammer to shape or bend strips of metal, pound a rivet or flatten a pipe. Every shop needs an anvil, and the scrap yard, I thought, would be the place to get one cheaply. When I went in the office, the fellow behind the counter said there probably were lengths of old railroad tracks somewhere in the yard, but I would have to look for a piece myself. When I walked out into the scrap yard, I avoided getting near the big crane that was piling up scrap iron using a magnet on the end of its cables. It took me only a few minutes to find a 10-foot length of track, much too heavy for me to handle. I went back toward the office and told a worker what I needed. He jumped on a skid loader, picked up the track, and cut off a 12-inch piece with his acetylene torch. After stopping at the office and paying the clerk a few dollars, I was on my way with the latest tool for my growing collection.

I took the task of building a collection of tools for the homestead seriously. Early on, in one of the magazines, I read an article on "the essential tools and implements" for a homestead shop and went down the list of 106 tools the author recommended. In some cases, I already had the tools, but in most instances I needed to buy them at the local hardware store, order them from a catalog, find them at rummage sales, or, in the case of the anvil, make do with recycled materials. It soon became clear to me that if you need to buy a particular tool, you should buy the best you can afford, use it properly, take care of it by maintaining it, and, when not using it, put it in a place where you will find it the next time you need it. That seems pretty obvious, I suppose, but I don't always proceed in that fashion, and sometimes I've done just the opposite. Worse, on at least a couple of occasions, I've misplaced a tool and had to buy another to replace it, only finding it later behind some boards or on a window sill in the barn. Then, I would own two – when I only need one. That's careless and wasteful, and, of course, fully human. When you are focused on a job and working hard to get it finished, it's easy to overlook the necessity of picking up all your tools after a job and putting them back where you got them. Instead, you want to put what you just fixed into use and get back to the other later. When it comes to tools, I have a bad habit involving something every homesteader carries with him: A good, sharp jackknife. I've lost two since coming to Hiram Hill, and I think I know what happens. I get busy with a project and put down my knife, leaving it there and forgetting where I left it. This likely happens when I am doing a job like cutting twine to repair a hole in the plastic fencing around our apple trees or cutting out weeds that have wrapped around the power take-off shaft on my tractor. When it comes time to use the knife again, I reach in my pocket to no avail. That doesn't make me happy, and I hate plunking down $12 or $14 dollars for another Buck knife when I know, somewhere, the first one is rusting in the tall grass.

Kathy had a bad habit of leaving her garden tools where she dropped them when she was done weeding or planting, and it irritated me when I would have to round up the tools and return them to the garden shed. But I tried to avoid any confrontation over this because I was grateful that she was doing the weeding in the garden, a job I loathe and do only when I must. Kathy, on the other hand, truly enjoys the task, and it is common in the spring and summer to see her on her hands and knees pulling weeds between rows of beans, radishes, lettuce, and spinach, with Cooper lying in the dirt watching her. At different times I've brought up the subject of putting tools back where they belong, and to her credit, Kathy now takes greater care in doing that. Of course, she has caught me ignoring my own rules more than once, so I make sure I never become too righteous about this matter.

Buying good tools that don't disappoint you the first time you use them is a must. I've learned a lesson on this subject, as well. When digging out rocks, I generally use a spade and pry bar. My shovel always performs admirably. The handle is strong, and the blade can stand up to some rough use. Not so with my pry bar. I paid $25 for it at a farm fleet store and knew I was taken the first time I tried to pry up a big rock. The shaft bends under force, not like the stout bar my dad used on our farm. I still use mine today for prying, and its opposite end is useful for tamping around posts, but sometimes I think I need to make another trip to the scrap yard and find something better.

There are dozens of tools needed in a shop, and you acquire them as you perform the various repair and construction tasks at hand. But once I began working on Hiram Hill, I deliberately went about assembling a group of tools that I knew would be needed for heavy work sooner or later. These included a sledge hammer, splitting maul, camping ax, pole saw, bow saw, crow bar, wrecking bar, bench vise, post-hole digger, steel fence post driver, pitch fork, and potato fork. I purchased these tools at hardware and farm supply stores, watching for sales and buying the best quality product on the racks.

Never knowing what the next repair job will be, I keep a roll of stove pipe wire and a supply of string, rope, twine, and duct tape on hand for a multitude of jobs. A glue gun, heavy duty stapler, and plenty of steel wool and sandpaper also are necessities. Having a large steel dust pan and a heavy-duty shop broom makes cleanup in the shop go easier. I prefer a traditional kitchen-type broom over a push broom. Homesteaders also need a piece of old galvanized pipe to use as a "cheater" bar on the end of a wrench when a nut refuses to budge. A log chain, tie-down straps and cords, and a come-along device also will quickly prove their value.

My pole saw is worth mentioning. I bought it out of a professional landscaping and gardening supply catalog, and it is superior to the pole saws with ropes that you find in the hardware stores, although more pricey. This one comes in two six-foot sections with a "turbo" type cutting head that rips its way through limbs quickly. Good tools are worth every penny you pay for them.

My 24x28-foot shop is compact but entirely sufficient for my needs. One side serves as my woodworking and general repair area and houses most of my hand tools and power equipment, as well as several work tables. The other half of the building, in addition to providing a parking stall for my pickup, serves as a vehicle service area and a place to work on the lawn mowers and other small engine equipment. I heat the shop with my wood-burning stove, I so am able to work there in comfort year around.

As time went on, I began to develop more homesteading skills, but in two areas – sharpening and tying knots – progress has been limited. No matter how hard

I try, I never seem to put a really sharp edge on kitchen knives, garden tools, chisels, and even my own jackknife. I've got an assortment of sharpening stones and have read several articles on sharpening techniques, but success has eluded me. My efforts probably get a passing grade, but no gold stars. A friend gave me an old electric motor, and I mounted a grinding stone on it. It works well for sharpening mower blades, so I have some success there. I also use an eight-inch mill bastard file for sharpening the ends of my shovels, garden hoe and loppers. When out in the woods cutting firewood, I usually touch up my chainsaw chains with a round file to keep them sharp, but eventually I take them to a small engine shop for a precise sharpening.

Tying good knots also is a challenge for me, and I went so far as to buy a book on the subject. While watching TV, I would work with a piece of cord, practicing slip, bowline, sheet bend, and hitch knots. The problem is that I don't use some of the knots enough to remember them when a situation calls for a particular kind. My friend, Phil, was a Boy Scout. The Scout leaders taught him to tie an array of knots, and Phil still puts them into use today. So, when we are working on a project together, I gladly defer to him when we need to tie a special type of knot.

There came a point on our homestead journey when I thought we had too many small gasoline engines on the place. At one time, we had a push mower, riding mower, old riding mower with the cutting deck removed, snow blower, wood splitter, garden tiller, generator, chainsaw, and power weed whip. These things perform important jobs, but they require regular maintenance if they are going to run when you pull the starter rope. The old, used tiller I bought gave out and wasn't replaced because now my friend, Ferris, comes over with his tiller each spring and works up our ground. The old riding mower is gone, too, after the engine gave out. We originally bought it for $300 secondhand to mow grass, but eventually got a new mower. I took the worn-out mower deck off the old one, and we bought a little trailer to put behind it. Kathy used it regularly for several years when doing garden and landscaping work around the place. Finally, the weed whip never worked very well, so it has been retired. That means we have three fewer small engines to worry about now. That's OK with me.

The best tool on our place is the Ford 8N tractor, our homestead workhorse that, like the Energizer bunny, just keeps going. Over the years, I have assembled several pieces of equipment to attach to the back of the tractor. These include a carry-all platform that allows me to load rocks, bales, lumber, and all sorts of things on the back of the tractor to haul where needed, and a disk, road blade, snow blower, and brush hog. I can tow the wood splitter with it, haul brush and firewood in a trailer behind it, and drag logs out of the woods.

When the 4x4 post holding our wood duck house fell over into our pond, I was able to get close enough with the tractor to hook a chain on the post and pull it out of the ground and pond, so I could set it up at another spot. Without the help of the tractor, I would have struggled to accomplish the task and more likely would have had to saw the post in two, leaving part of it in the soft, brushy embankment. The tractor and equipment also allow me to be of service to our neighbors, when they need their roads graded or gardens worked up. If I hook up the blade to the tractor and take off down the road to the neighbor's place, you can bet the dogs will be running ahead to get in on the action.

Having tools means I can make things, and there is great satisfaction when I can build something that we can use in the house or outside. One day Ferris called me to say that a friend of his had an old boat trailer to give away and asked me whether I wanted it. He knew I was interested in acquiring a flat-bed trailer and told me that I could convert the boat trailer into one. Good idea, I said. My old Apache trailer still was in great shape, but it has fixed sides and can't be used to haul a riding lawn mower or similar equipment that needs to be driven onto the trailer. Soon, Ferris came with the boat trailer, stopping first at the county recycling center to dispose of the old fiberglass boat that came with it. So, I ended up with a good, serviceable boat trailer for the recycling fee of $30. After removing all the braces and rollers that were in place to accommodate the boat, I built a deck atop the steel framework and added slide-in sides for the box. The trailer came with a long tongue, which I shortened. After repacking the wheel bearings and giving it a paint job, I now have a fine, sturdy trailer for hauling. Best of all, the trailer box tilts up when a steel pin is removed, which helps when unloading sand, dirt, or compost.

When driving by a small woodworking business one day, I noticed what looked like a flagpole leaning against the back of the building. Thereafter, I would take note of it each time I passed until, finally, I got up the nerve to inquire whether it might be for sale. I wanted to set up a flagpole at our rock pile, but always was deterred by the cost of a new pole. The owner of the business told me the flagpole had fallen over, and its bent, damaged end had been cut off. But if I wanted it, I could have it. To make the pole longer, I went to a second-hand place and bought a six-foot piece of well casing, burying one end in the ground in concrete. This left the casing extended above the ground about three feet. I filled the casing with concrete and slipped in the bottom end of the smaller-diameter pole deep enough to secure it. Earlier, I had put a fresh coat of paint on both the pole and casing. I raised Old Glory and felt happy with the new addition to our yard. Adding to the good feeling was the fact that at the second-hand market, I found a brass ball that once was on a bedpost. I mounted the ball atop the pole to give it a traditional look.

Early in our homesteading adventure, I noticed a medium-size wooden electric cable spool had been dumped in a construction site fire pit that I had visited several times. I fished it out of there before the workers burned it, took it home, and, using the spool placed on its side as a pedestal, built a sturdy work table that sits in my shop today. I also bought a half-dozen used interior doors from a lady for a couple of bucks each. The doors made good tops for several tables I built.

When we moved to Hiram Hill in 1997, my wood-working power equipment consisted of a skill saw, table saw, miter saw, router, and palm sander. The miter saw was a new purchase and a godsend when I took on the job of building our kitchen cabinets. Before then, a skill saw was my main tool when it came to building furni-ture. I chose to build with pine because it was relatively inexpensive and easy to work with. It gave us the choice of finishing the surfaces with varnish or paint.

As the house was going up, we priced ready-made kitchen cabinets. The estimates always were sobering, running from $4,500 on up. Finally, while riding in the pickup one day on our way back home, I told Kathy that I thought I could build the cabinets myself. The more we talked about it, the more doable it sounded. Our purpose was to build plain, simple, and functional furni-ture and cabinets that would serve us well and last many years. And, then, after making the decision to build the cabinets ourselves, we received a pleasant surprise.

We had hired a contractor to install tongue-and-grooved pine boards on the vaulted ceiling over the living and dining rooms. We had the ceiling vaulted to create as much space as possible around the masonry heater, which sits between the two rooms. To our delight, we found that the ceiling workers left a pile of pine board ends that had been cut off – mostly in three-foot lengths. Suddenly, we had material for our cabinet doors and for the door on our laundry chute. When the cabinet project was finished, our total cost for material and hardware amounted to a little more than $400. It was worth the effort.

Except for the two cabinets I built for our shop, I never had made kitchen cabinets before. But what I learned about building cabinets and such things as vanities, dressers, armoires, and chests, is that, in most cases, you first build a box and then put doors on it or construct drawers. You also need to add some trim to cover screw heads and seams, as well as make it attractive. But finding a way to join the parts of a cabinet together proved to be a challenge. I didn't have the tools or experience to try more sophisticated joinery, such as using dowels or making dove-tail cuts. Watching woodworker Norm Abram do his magic on *The New Yankee Workshop* is a pleasure, but his skills far exceed mine.

I solved the joinery problem by using 1 1/4-inch wide wood blocks. I glued the blocks to the tops, sides, and bottoms of the cabinet boxes and secured them with drywall screws. The blocks, cut the same length as the 12-inch-wide cabinet boards, fit into the inside corners of the boxes. If shelves were needed, I also supported them with blocks, glue and screws. I added trim pieces, usually with mitered corners, over the exposed ends of the blocks and the cabinet's front edges to give the cabinet an attractive, finished appearance. These I fastened with glue and finishing nails. Next, I assembled the doors with the tongue-and-grooved pine boards, fastening them together on the back with more wooden blocks. The trim pieces serve as the mounting plates for the cabinet door hinges. I built the counter cabinets using the same techniques. When drawers were needed, I used particle board to make the actual drawers and then attached pine boards on the front ends before putting on handles. Next, I added drawer rollers purchased at the hardware store. After a little router work on the edges of the drawer fronts, the drawers were ready for varnish.

After the cabinets were made, I built a bookcase that covers the east wall of the living room. The bookcase consists of two sets of shelves on either side of a large bay window, joined together at the top by a shelf running the entire width of the room. Extra deep shelves on each side provide a place for our TV and stereo. With the exception of our dining room table and living room furniture, I built almost everything else in our house, including:

Office computer desk, shelves and cabinets

Office bookcase

2 bathroom vanities

Headboard for master bedroom

Armoire with drawers

Bedroom "cedar" chest

Chest of drawers

Vegetable bin

Mudroom glove/cap case

Firewood box

Kindling box

I used three-quarter-inch pine boards for virtually all the projects. In building these things ourselves, we had the advantage of sizing them to fit a particular space. Kathy assisted me at certain times and did most of the varnishing. None of what I made is going to win any prizes, and I always tell people not to look too closely lest they spot a flaw. Kathy told me that when the Amish make something, they deliberately build in a flaw somewhere just to affirm that only God is perfect.

I can assure everyone that my work exceeds that particular Amish standard.

12

DIGGING A POND, BUILDING A BARN

O n a warm, sunny day in July 2007, a young man drove up in a car and came to our door. He said he was an intern working with the state Department of Natural Resources (DNR) and wanted to take a picture of a particular wetland that was supposedly located on our property. Immediately, I thought he meant the big pond we overlook on our hill, but he assured me that wasn't it. I then told him there was a small, eyebrow-shaped pond located just beyond our southern boundary — would that be it? No, he said, the pond was approximately 400 feet from the house and on our property.

His comment flew over me again, and all I could say was, "Well, then you must mean the big pond back on the county land to the southwest."

"No, sir," he said. "The pond I am looking for is

here." He held up his Global Positioning System (GPS) device, and showing up on the little screen were not only the three ponds I had just mentioned, none of which is on our property, but also a fourth, tiny one – our own little pond that we had dug a few years before!

"Oh, my goodness – do you mean the little pond we dug over there?" I said, pointing through the trees.

"Yes, that must be it. It's 400 feet from your house."

We walked over to the pond, and I explained to him that we had gotten a permit to dig it out in 2003. He wasn't concerned about any of that. All he wanted to do was take a picture of the pond because DNR officials had spotted it on satellite pictures and didn't have a record of it.

Big brother was watching, I guess. Bill and Kathy had made their mark on this world.

Making that mark didn't come easily. But the result proved to be one of the best things we have done to improve our property. The pond is located on the south edge of what we call the West Meadow, an area that was completely hidden by trees and brush when we first explored the land. Coming off our hill, we had to slip through a thicket of hazel and enter an area with numerous mature oak trees leading to a little meadow beyond. On the south edge of this meadow, a dense stand of alder surrounded the northern tip of a long, narrow wetland that cuts through the forty. We dug our pond at the tip of this wetland.

I didn't see the possibility of a pond there that first year, but, later, as I walked the land, it became evident to me that this would be a good spot. In addition to the alder, several small oak trees, and a nice, big birch were positioned on the edge of the wetland. Except for spring and during exceptionally wet periods, the wetland didn't have standing water in it. But it always was marshy and covered with sedge grasses. Kathy told me later that she never could see what I saw when I would show her the area. She said there were too many bushes and trees in the way for her to visualize a pond.

We had the pond dug in 2001, but a few years before, I had signed up for the Woodland Stewardship Program operated by the DNR. The stewardship program is a way for the DNR to work with private landowners in forested areas to help them manage their woodlands and wetlands. A DNR forester came by, and we walked through the property from one end to the other. He estimated the numbers of trees and logging potential for each type of tree, and we sat down to discuss what my particular goals were for the land. Did I plan to have parts of it logged off at some point? What wildlife species would I like to attract? Did I plan to plant any more trees?

Following his visit and our discussions, the forester drew up a Woodland Stewardship Plan for our 43 acres, first allowing me to review a draft and make comments before a final version was produced. Along with a copy of the plan and a couple of aerial photos of the land, the DNR also gave me a big binder containing valuable information on managing forests, building trails, planting and harvesting trees, nurturing wildlife, and much more. Thousands of small landowners in Minnesota have taken advantage of the program, and in March 2003, Kathy and I attended a conference in Duluth celebrating the fact that more than a million acres of private land in the state had been enrolled in the program.

Our plans to dig a wildlife pond figured prominently in our stewardship plan, so I began to look into what was involved in such a venture. I had hoped to have the pond dug in 2000, but because of money concerns, I decided to wait until 2001. That January, I called an official from the county Soil and Water Conservation

District office to find out what I had to do to make it happen. He came out, and I showed him the place where I hoped the pond could be dug. He said I had picked a good spot, and we discussed what the pond might look like. It appeared to both of us that a pond similar in shape to the number eight would work best. In effect, there would be two small ponds, one slightly larger than the other, connected by a neck of water between the two. The design accommodated a large birch tree, which would be situated at the narrowing of the pond.

A week or so later, the county official sent me a drawing of the proposed pond that he had worked up. It was now time to get permits from the state and county and proceed with the work. Fortunately, the Soil and Water Conservation office gave me a few names of people who had dug other ponds in the county, and I picked one and gave him a call. Richard had dug many ponds before with his dragline and gave me an estimate of $1,300 for the .3 acre pond I was contemplating. So, before I knew it, we were ready to go, and all I had to do was wait for Richard to show up and start digging.

Kathy will never forget his arrival.

One day in June, Richard drove up our drive in

his roaring truck, pulling a low-boy trailer on which his 1946-vintage dragline with a 40-foot boom rode. He stopped just in time to avoid making a big hole in our shop's overhead garage door with his boom, which stuck out well beyond the truck's nose. Kathy, watching this scene through the kitchen sink window, was aghast and yelled at me as I was going out the door, "How is he supposed to get that thing down there? He'll never get that through the trees! Did you see? He almost hit the shop!"

I can't remember what I was thinking, but I was glad he had finally arrived. Richard jumped out of the truck, and we shook hands. We talked for a while, and then I showed him the drawing for the pond. We walked around the shop and then down the slope on a new road I had cut out through the trees to get to the West Meadow. Kathy's concerns were real because it was all problematic whether the dragline with its long boom could be maneuvered through this maze. But I was prepared to take out more trees if necessary, so we continued walking on to the pond site.

By then, I had cut down all the alder surrounding the north side of the wetland, so Richard would have easy access. I wasn't concerned about the alder on the other side because he could remove the growth with the dragline's bucket. Just cutting down the trees took a couple of days of hard work with my chainsaw. I let the alder lay where I cut it, and Richard later covered it all up with the soil dug from the bottom of the wetland.

Everything looked OK, so Richard and I went back to the yard. A half-hour later, he had the dragline unloaded from the trailer and began making his way around the shop and down the slope to the meadow. He had to turn the boom right and then left as the machine moved ahead on its big tracks, but before long he was headed straight down the passageway between the trees and into the meadow. The dragline's tracks tore up the grass in many places, but otherwise no damage was done and no other trees had to be removed. Kathy was relieved, and I think she began to see that there was no turning back now.

After parking the dragline, Richard returned to the yard, got in his truck, and backed down the driveway. Before leaving, he told us he would be back after the Fourth of July to start digging, and it probably would take him two or three days to finish the job. We were just going with the flow regarding all this because we really didn't have a clue what to expect.

True to his promise, Richard showed up as he said, and began to dig with his big machine. We soon came to appreciate his skill at working the dragline. The machine's bucket was hooked to long cables running off the boom, and Richard deftly flung the bucket where he wanted it and dug away at the earth. The permits allowing me to dig out the wetland required that all soil removed – called spoil – had to be placed away from the pond's banks, and once the pond was dug, grass had to be seeded on the spoil and around the pond to prevent erosion.

On the second day, the pond was taking shape nicely, but Richard's dragline broke down. A link broke in a big, four-inch-wide chain that drives the dragline's tracks, leaving the machine mired in deep, watery muck and leaning to one side. Richard didn't seem too concerned, and I gathered that this wasn't the first time the chain had broken. Yet, I couldn't imagine trying to fix it myself in such dreadful conditions. He's going to have to get a bulldozer or something to pull the dragline out to high ground, I thought. Richard had other plans. He stepped into the muck, crawled under the machine, and, lying on his back in the mud, began to remove the broken link. He asked me to hand him his tools as needed. After removing the old link, he had to pull the heavy, mud-covered chain tight enough to get the new link in. He somehow managed to get the chain back on the track's sprockets. It took about an hour of hard work, but he got it all back together again. Soon, he was back at the dragline controls, pivoting the machine on its tracks so that he could back it out of its precarious place and resume digging.

The next day, Richard drove the dragline away from the excavation site and parked it in a grassy area near our pig pen. He was finished, leaving us with a large dug-out area with standing water on the bottom and a mess of spoil all around the excavated site. He left the dragline there for two months before coming back to get it – after a couple of reminder calls from me.

By the time he returned to get his machine, we had made considerable progress in grooming the pond area. There still wasn't much water in it, but Richard said that, come spring, it should fill completely. I had to hire a fellow to come in with his small dozer to spread out the spoil more evenly. Using my tractor, I disked the whole area and ran a drag over it numerous times. Finally, I seeded it with a mix of timothy, ryegrass, and clover and covered the seeded areas with straw. It was beginning to look better, and we could see the possibilities.

The next spring the pond filled up, just as Richard had predicted, and sedge grasses and blue flag iris began to grow along the water's edge. New shoots of willows and alder also appeared, and I planted a few spruce seedlings along one side. I pushed some big rocks down to the edge of the water for turtles to sit on in the summer. Our first ducks showed up, and now, at one time or another, mallards, teal, and wood ducks fly in. A pair of Canadian geese shows up every spring, and peepers and leopard frogs create a din. Turtles sun themselves on the rocks, and slip into the water if we get too close. A few water-lily pads float on the water. I built a park bench and set it up near the pond, and it's a favorite place of mine now.

A couple of years later, I built a 32-foot-long footbridge across one end of the pond to give us easy access to a trail on the other side. The bridge consists of four, eight-foot sections of tamarack planking that sit on piers resembling hurdles used at track meets. The modular design allows me to remove one section at a time if needed, yet it is strong enough to support the riding lawnmower when I'm crossing over to mow trails.

For several winters I used my walk-behind snow

blower to clear a rink on the frozen pond, and the neighbor kids came over to skate. Afterward, we invited them to come in from the cold for hot chocolate and cookies.

With the pond completed, our thoughts now turned to another major project we had discussed many times over early-morning coffee – a barn for Hiram Hill. It, too, was part of a three-fold plan for the West Meadow: First, a pond, followed by a barn, and then an orchard. I couldn't plant apple trees before I built the barn because I needed to move dirt in the open areas where the apple trees would be planted to create a suitable building site for the barn. So, it was first things first.

We built our barn in 2002, the summer after the pond was dug, but we knew what kind of barn we were going to build several years before that. Monte Burch's book, *Building Small Barns, Sheds & Shelters* (Storey Publishing, 1982) has several good plans for attractive barns, but one in particular caught our eye – a 24x32-foot saltbox style pole barn with wood siding. The barn features a loft on one side with access from the outside, a small door on the front, several windows, and a pair of large, sliding doors. It seemed perfect for us. We didn't intend to put animals in the barn. Rather, we needed a place for the tractor, wood splitter, and riding lawn mower, as well as storage space for straw bales, pig feed, ladders, and odds and ends. It's a handsome design, and I studied it carefully, read every word about it multiple times, and tried to understand the sketchy plans provided as best I could. I decided that I would add a second small door on the back.

A few months before we began construction in May, I contacted James, who operates a small lumber mill on his place a couple of miles east of us, to see whether he would saw the boards I would need to build the barn. He agreed to do the job, and we settled on a price. He soon cut all the lumber I had ordered and stacked it up for drying on his place. When it came time to start framing the structure at the end of May, I took my tractor and my neighbor Fred's flat-bed trailer over to James's place and loaded up the beautiful white pine lumber, making two trips. Paying James was a pleasure. He did a great job sawing the 2x4s, 2x6s, 2x8s and 2x10s. I grew to love working with white pine. It is soft, yet very strong, and it is easy to cut and shape.

On May 5, a local excavator came in with his bulldozer and pushed up dirt for a level building site. I hired another person with a skid loader and post-hole digger to dig the holes I had marked for the 5-by-6 posts. Once that was done, my friends, Curt and Jack, helped me place all the posts and set them in concrete. We were on our way, I told Kathy, and the fun was just starting.

Following the building plan in Monte Burch's book and making my own adaptations as I went along, I started driving long, pole-barn nails into the white pine planks I hoisted up between the posts. I found that by using some quick-release clamps I had purchased, I could place one end of a 2x10 plank on a post, hold it there with a clamp, and then go to the other end, lift it up, and nail it in place. If it got too dicey, I would call on Kathy to hold the other end, but for the most part I went about the work alone, day after day. It soon came time to put up the rafters, and I needed Kathy's help for certain. She gamely grabbed the ends of the 20-foot, 2x10 rafters and lifted them into place, while I situated the other end and started nailing. We got them all up, but the 20-footers only reached part of the way, and we still needed to put up a ridge pole at the top of the building. For that job, we sought the help of another friend, Derek, and his carpentry experience helped greatly as we finished connecting all the rafters to the long ridge pole running along the peak of the roof.

A few days later, I began to feel exhausted, and it was everything I could do to get out of bed. I thought maybe I had sun stroke from spending so much time outside working on the barn. I later discovered, after a fruitless trip to a hospital emergency room, that I had contracted Lyme disease from a deer tick. Kathy drove me to the emergency room because my temperature had spiked to 105, and I was battling fever and chills alternately. The doctor there didn't find anything, and I went home, took Tylenol to reduce the fever and hoped to ride this thing out. The next day, Kathy noticed a big, red blotch on my back surrounding what looked like a tick bite, and we suspected Lyme disease immediately. So, we went to a local doctor, who gave me a 30-day prescription for an antibiotic.

It took a week before I started to feel better. Frustrated at the slow progress and not looking forward to the big job of roofing the barn, I called Kevin, the contractor who built our house, and asked him if he could send out a crew and do the job. To my pleasant surprise, his men came out in the morning a couple of days later and finished the job by three in the afternoon. I felt relieved, but didn't like the fact that the cost would increase significantly because of the hired work.

The summer days passed, and I kept working, installing the floor in the loft, and framing in the windows and doors. Soon, Kathy and I started putting on the three-quarter-inch thick rough sawn plywood siding and accompanying battens, with Derek helping us hoist up the uppermost panels. We painted all the trim boards before putting them up, and then we stained the barn a New England barn red. I made all the doors myself, and after hanging them, our project was complete. It was August 27.

In my shop the next winter, I built a cupola for the barn, and Kathy, Derek, and I lifted it up to the roof one nice spring day. We struggled to raise it, and for a moment I thought we were going to drop it, but fortunately we prevailed. After cutting a hole in the roof, we slipped it in and installed the flashing. When that was done, I mounted a rooster weather vane on top given to us by Kathy's mother and dad.

Fred said the barn will stand a hundred years. That made me feel proud. It's a remarkably solid structure. In many places I not only drove in pole-barn nails to secure braces and supports, I also glued them with construction adhesive. But, unless the next person who comes along on Hiram Hill sees to it that the roof stays leakproof, even our barn will weaken and eventually fall in, just like my dad's pole barn did when the owners of my family's former farm let the buildings deteriorate before their eyes. I've come to realize that what's important to me may not be important to the next person, so now is the time to enjoy what my hands have made, and let come what may.

Enjoy we did. In late September, we hosted a group of friends for a barn warming, hired a music maker from a nearby town to entertain us, and ate a dinner primarily made from food grown on our place – ham from the pigs we had butchered earlier that fall; potatoes and broccoli from the garden; and bread, raspberry jam, and pickles we had made ourselves. Kathy also baked some pumpkin bars for dessert.

That little party remains a happy memory.

13

DOGS AND OTHER CRITTERS

When we first came to Hiram Hill, I mentioned to Kathy that I would like to get an "outside dog," meaning one bigger than Cooper who would follow me around on the property and make his presence known, so various critters in the woods – mainly deer – would stay away from the garden and flower beds. I told Kathy I wanted to name the dog, Riley.

As events unfolded, I never found a dog I could call Riley. Instead, two black labs named Tara and Buddy found me, and they became two of my best friends. The dogs lived across the pond, and when our neighbors and their children moved away, they came to live with us. It wasn't like we were strangers because for several years they came over to our place early each morning and stayed the whole day, while the neighbors were at work and the kids were at school. In the evening, I would clap my hands and tell the dogs, "It's time to go home." Immediately, without the slightest hesitation, they would turn and head down the path they had worn between our place and their home.

I once had planned to build a footbridge over the beaver channel in the wetland surrounding the big pond. I figured the bridge would be necessary for an easy passage to the field beyond and our neighbor's place. But the dogs found a better route along an old, overgrown beaver dam that blocks one end of the beaver channel and prevents water in the pond from draining out into an adjoining small pond near Beaver Point. Once we saw the path the dogs had blazed, we cut brush out along it, and now we have a clear path between the two properties through the trees and brush and across the field.

Buddy was Tara's pup, and we suspect the father of her litter was Ace, Fred's dog down the lane. Before Buddy came along, Tara ran with another dog the neighbors owned – Bree, a Brittany spaniel. She and Tara loved to roam the area, and each morning as I looked out our window across the field, I would see them leave the neighbor's grove of pines and willows and start their morning excursion. Bree died a couple of years after we moved to Hiram Hill. Tara ran alone for a while, coming by our place each day for a biscuit and some attention, and later she had a litter of pups. One day while we were working in the garden, we heard Cooper barking and looked around to see what was the matter. Coming up the hill on the path was Tara, followed by her six pups, including Buddy. She wanted to show us her beautiful babies. The pups rollicked in the grass for a while and then she took them home again.

The neighbor boy wanted to keep one pup and chose Buddy. The dog soon grew up and became Tara's constant companion. The two ran together fluidly, as if they were harnessed and knew instinctively which way they would turn and what they would do next. Tara groomed Buddy often, licking his face and ears, while Buddy laid back and enjoyed the attention. When it became apparent that the dogs would need another home, Kathy and some of our friends, who knew and loved Buddy and Tara as much as we did, prevailed upon me to offer to take them. The neighbors were relieved, I think, and after they agreed, I made it a point on the day we took them in to tell the two dogs that they could stay with us now. Kathy said it was the tone of my voice that made them react the way they did, but whatever it was, the two animals took off running side by side at top speed across the lawn and into the tall grass and weeds. As they ran, they jumped up and body slammed each other, growling and pretending to be fighting. Then they fell back to the ground, stumbled and rolled in the tall grass, only to get up again and take off in another direction, barking and slamming into each other, as if they were saying, "Oh, happy days! We get to stay!"

That day, I made them a temporary place to sleep in our house garage, which they called home immediately. Later, I made them a lean-to dog house in one corner of the garage using the remaining canvas we had salvaged from the Apache camper for one side. Buddy especially loved the little corner doghouse. When our friend's golden lab trotted into the garage and tried to enter the tent, Buddy would have none of that and ran the golden lab out unceremoniously. It was the only time I ever heard him snarl and threatened harm.

One time when I went into the barn, Buddy followed, but when I left, I closed the door, inadvertently locking him inside. An hour or so later, I asked Kathy if she had seen Buddy. We called a few times, but he didn't come. We called some more. Both Cooper and Tara seemed concerned as well, and finally Cooper started toward the barn. He would stop and look back at me, as if to say, "Come on, I know where Buddy is." He ran straight for the barn door, and when I opened it, Buddy came out wagging his tail, and all three dogs had to touch noses to acknowledge that everything was OK. Buddy never made a sound while in the barn, even though he could hear us, obviously. We made a big deal of the situation and said, "Buddy was lost! We didn't know where Buddy was! But now we found him!" That would send Tara and Buddy off running and body slamming again. They couldn't contain the good feeling welling up in them at being the absolute center of attention. They had to take off running at full speed to deal with all this commotion.

I once took a picture of Tara and Buddy that, I think, perfectly captures their personalities. Holding dog biscuits in one hand and the camera in the other, I snapped a picture that shows Tara standing bright eyed and eager to grab her biscuit, and Buddy, sitting and waiting for the treat. Buddy was timid and always preferred to stand back and let Tara take the lead. I cut a foot-long piece of old plastic garden hose to play fetch with the dogs, but Buddy wouldn't have anything to do with the game. Tara loved running after the hose when I threw it, but

Buddy would dart back in his tent in the garage when he saw what was going to happen. Likewise, when the new neighbor kids came to play hockey on our pond ice, Tara loved to chase after the puck as it slid across the ice, tumbling into the snow banks on the sides. But not Buddy. No, he preferred to sit off to the side and watch. Hockey was just too violent a game for him.

But sometimes Buddy's instincts got the better of him. He once ran off with a female dog in the neighborhood that had been abandoned by some residents who had recently left the area. The woman who owned the dog also had kept a couple of horses that occasionally broke loose from their corral and had to be rounded up. Fred suspected the animals didn't have enough food, and at least once he brought over a large, round bale of hay for them. On two different mornings one fall, I looked out the window and two horses were grazing on our lawn, their droppings scattered throughout the yard. I knew they belonged to the woman, and I also knew they had been loose for a while because I had seen them several times on our former neighbor's place across the pond. No one was living there at the time, so I didn't think too much of it. I also saw the woman's dog over there a few times. When I mentioned this to the school bus driver one day, he told me that the woman and her children had left their place more than a month ago. The horses and dog were fending for themselves. I called the sheriff's office to inform them of the situation, but it took two weeks before they could find someone to take the horses and deal with the dog.

In the meantime, the female dog went into heat, and Buddy caught scent of it. He hung with her for a couple of days, after which I finally coaxed him into the pickup, took him home and put him in our fenced chicken run. We had butchered the chickens that fall, and were planning to get a new batch of chicks in the spring, so Buddy had the place to himself. That night, though, he broke out of the run and headed back over to his female friend. The next day, a sheriff's deputy came by and told me he was going to try to find the female dog and put it down because he had no other options. I watched from the hill as he drove to our neighbor's place next door. There, I could see Buddy and the other dog. The deputy fired his gun, trying to hit the female, but all I saw was Buddy in a dead run heading south into the woods beyond. We couldn't find Buddy after that, although we drove the roads, walked our trails and called out his name frequently. Two days passed without finding him. The next day, just after Kathy left for school, I stood on the hill and called several times once again. Cooper and Tara were outside with me. Finally, I told myself I would make one last search to see if I could find Buddy. The two other dogs trotted along beside me as I walked down the trails. When I got almost to the edge of our property, where the trail turns and goes up a hill in the woods, Cooper barked and ran up the trail with Tara behind him. There was Buddy, standing at the top of the hill with his tail wagging, unsure if he were in trouble or not. But, I yelled, "Buddy! We've found you! Good boy!" The dogs, with their tails in a full wag, had to touch noses and bark their approval. Buddy followed me home and never left on such a venture again – perhaps because the very next morning he was in the pickup with me heading to the vet in Bemidji for neutering surgery.

I never found out whether the deputy's bullet hit the female dog, but the next summer, the new owners of the place where the woman with the horses had lived found the remains of the animal in a pile of junk within an old barn that had long ago collapsed. I wondered whether the dog had been wounded and took shelter there before dying. Rural life can be beautiful, but it can

overnight, but the next morning the dog and I were on our way to a vet's office in the next county, which took in strays for the humane society there. At the time Tara and Buddy were coming over to our place every day, so I didn't need another dog.

Another time, though, I would have done differently. A mid-size mixed breed dog showed up in our yard, also in the fall. My tractor was parked in one of the wood shed's stalls, and I found the dog curled up in the padded seat. He was frightened when I approached and growled at me. I talked to him a while, but he remained scared, so I thought I would leave him alone for the time being. When I went back later to check on him, he had left, and I never saw him again. I was disappointed because I had been having some pleasant thoughts about befriending the dog and taking him in. I would have named him Riley.

Strays and runaway horses are not the only visitors we get on our homestead. At one time or another deer, bears, beavers, groundhogs, foxes, rabbits, skunks, raccoons, pocket gophers, red squirrels, chipmunks, mice, and voles have stirred our ire. We know we must share the woods and fields with the creatures of the wild, but sometimes we resent it when they encroach on our immediate domain.

The first time I set up our pig pen in the West Meadow, I placed our old well hut next to it for storing pig feed. We didn't use the hut anymore because the well's pressure tank no longer sat outside, but was in our basement. A black bear tore the door off its hinges one night to get at the feed bags. We could only imagine that the two little pigs in the adjacent shelter buried themselves deep in the straw and didn't make a sound while the bear did his deed. Once, Kathy came across a bear in our yard about 100 feet away. She was walking toward our storage shed and spotted the bear crossing the yard in front of the wood shed. We also saw a bear while walking down the township road. Thereafter that summer, Kathy carried a coffee can containing a few empty rifle shell casings and shook the can now and then just to let any bears know she was in the area. While there are occasional sightings, bears for the most part keep to themselves. We try not to go out of our way to attract them. After having several bird feeders smashed by bears seeking food, we no longer set them out. The feeders draw bears to the yard, especially at night, and we think it's best not to push our luck.

Deer are an ongoing problem, of course. They

browse our apple trees, flowers, and plants in the garden, as well as nip the lead bud on our pine seedlings if we don't protect them. If we plant any kind of fruit tree or bush, the only way we can expect them to survive is to put a fence around them. And even then, we may lose the war. We had several nice Nanking cherry bushes that we protected with screens, but one winter, voles ate the bark off the shoots, and we lost them all.

It took three attempts to get apple trees to the point where they started to bear fruit. Before we moved to Hiram Hill, I had planted four semi-dwarf apple trees on our main hill, but didn't protect them, except for putting plastic spiral wraps on their trunks during the winter. The deer browsed them down to bare sticks, so I uprooted them and threw them on the burn pile. I planted three more apple trees near the big rock pile by our house, but neglected to wrap their trunks one winter, and voles girdled all three, killing them. Finally, in 2001, I planted two crabapple trees in the same spot and have kept them fenced and protected. Both are producing abundantly now. I followed up that success by getting quite serious about an orchard by our new barn. In 2003, I planted seven standard-size apple trees and two plum trees there, and all but one apple and one plum tree have done well and are starting to produce. The trees are protected by fences year-around and trunk wrap in the winter. Deer frequent the orchard to graze on the grass and occasionally nip an apple tree bud that sticks out of the fencing, but for the most part we have stymied them. Each November, my neighbor, Steve, sets up his deer stand in the trees surrounding the orchard. He has successfully bagged a deer there each time.

One dry summer, we came under attack of a different sort. A skunk visited the yard at night and dug up grubs that lived just below the roots of the grass. When dry conditions persist, grubs move closer to the surface and eat the roots of the grass, killing it. The sod rips up easily as a result. I saw the skunk a couple of times, and I had my rifle in my hand, but I was reluctant to shoot it and have us deal with the smell that likely would follow. I began to think more about the situation and told Kathy I wasn't going to kill the skunk. Rather, I just wanted it to continue digging up and eating the nasty grubs that were ruining the lawn. People try chemical treatments to get rid of grubs with uneven success, from what I understand. Besides, we are reluctant to use any kind of pesticide or herbicide and rarely do. After a few weeks, the skunk didn't come back. Apparently, he had eaten all the grubs. I then disked the areas where the grubs and skunk had done their work and seeded the ground at freezing time. The seed sat in the ground over winter and then germinated in the spring, and the lawn is looking much better. The skunk actually did me a favor. I would have had to reseed anyway, but the grubs would still have been down in the soil ready to do more damage.

I have already discussed one of the worst critters we deal with – the porcupine. Both Tara and Buddy learned painful lessons when they encountered the quill-covered creature. Before Tara was with us, she put her nose and face too close to a porcupine and ended up with dozens of quills in her nose, lips, mouth, and tongue. And when Buddy was with us, he unfortunately endured the same painful experience. Tara's quills were removed by the neighbors, but I couldn't get all of Buddy's taken out and took him to the vet, who sedated him and removed several from the roof of his mouth. Holding down a dog in pain while trying to pull out porcupine quills is not a pleasant task for either man or dog, and after a while, both become exhausted from the ordeal. I'm thankful we can turn to vets when needed. It's easier on the dog, as well.

For the most part, the homestead is a peaceful place, and we live in harmony with the natural world. Even when a pocket gopher starts digging up the lawn, moving across it like General Sherman in Georgia, sending up fresh mounds of dirt each morning, I don't get excited. They're doing what they do best, and that's really all I'm trying to do. I'll get on it and put a stop to his little march, but I'm not going sweat the small stuff anymore.

Kathy picking green beans, August 2007.

Bill with some of the first State Fair apples, 2007.

14

FOOD FOR THE TABLE

B efore we built the barn in 2003, we did a lot of other sawing and hammering to reach the goals we had listed in our master plan. No buildings came with the property, so if we needed a structure to help us accomplish our objectives, we had to build it. As money became available, we drove to the lumber yard to get building materials and went to work. In the case of the barn and the footbridge, I was able to buy lumber directly from my neighbor, James, who produced what I needed on his sawmill in his yard. Some of that lumber came from trees James had logged on his own property.

When we built the wood shed in 1994, I thought its two stalls would provide enough space for my firewood needs. Each stall holds about three cords of wood, enough for a typical burning season. I always had another pile of firewood sitting outside, so if I needed a little more, I would take from the outside pile so no firewood would be removed from the second stall. That wood was to be burned the next winter. I decided, however, that a three-year cycle would be better, meaning each year there would be two stalls of dry wood available, while I worked to replace the firewood that I had used the previous winter. So, in July of 2000, I decided to add a third stall by building a lean-to structure on the north end of the wood shed. Minnesota Governor Jesse Ventura thought taxpayers should get a sales tax rebate in 2000, and one day we got a check for $400 in the mail. Kathy immediately said, "Bill, there's your lean-to for the wood shed." The project cost $371.61, so Governor Ventura had sent back just enough.

The year before – in 1999 – I built an 8x8-foot chicken coop, fully insulating the floor, walls and ceiling, and putting in windows with screens for ventilation. When I tallied the construction cost at $1,069.23, Kathy gulped, but then duly noted that the first egg would be quite costly, while the ones thereafter would be much less. Even so, I never regretted the initial expense. Chickens need sufficient warmth and light to continue laying during the cold, dark days of winter. Insulation and the timer-controlled lighting in the coop helped keep us well supplied with eggs for the table, even when the days were short and frigid.

We also completed the basement projects we had planned, adding a combination office/bedroom in 1998 and a bathroom, bedroom, and storage room in 2000. At the end of 2002, the tally sheet of our investment in Hiram Hill looked like this:

TOTAL COSTS – 1993-2002

House	$87,807.86
Shop	10,196.41
Wood shed	1,114.74
Storage shed (trade)	1,100.00
Chicken coop	1,069.23
Wood shed lean-to	371.61
Basement office	1,507.60
Basement bath, bedroom, etc.	4,101.81
Pond	1,300.00
Barn	9,466.08
Subtotal	**$118,035.34**
Land, well, road, other	22,731.17
Travel expenses	2,889.84
Grand total	**$143,656.35**

Later on, we put down pavers for a patio in front of

the house and made a few other improvements, but by the end of 2002, we had pretty much completed all the construction we envisioned when we drew up our plan. We did so without borrowing any money and remained free of debt. We probably could recoup our investment if we ever sold the property, but now we both shrug our shoulders when the subject is brought up. It really doesn't matter. Our experiences are more valuable than the dollars we might get in a sale. And we have no plans to sell, anyway.

We now had everything in place, and we were busy working in our gardens, raising pigs, tending to our small flock of chickens, cutting wood, and putting up whatever food we could for our table.

By 2002, we were old hands at raising pigs. We had read books and articles on the subject, but, initially, neither of us had any experience working with them. We needed some basic knowledge to get started, but we didn't burden ourselves with too much knowledge, either. As in so many things, knowledge is important, but a person still needs to jump in and do it. Experience is a great teacher, too.

When we started, people didn't take us seriously and told us we would become attached to the little pigs we were raising, probably would give them names, and when it came time, would not be able to have them butchered or eat the pork. Well, they were right on the first two, but wrong on their last prediction. Indeed, we did become attached to each pair of pigs we raised, and we gave them names, which I recorded in my little note-book:

1997   Mr. Pigg and Miss Piggy Pretty

1998   Pork and Beans

1999   Spic and Spam

2000   Link and Patty

2001   Spot and Spotless

2002   Ida and Eva

2003   Hydrox and Oreo

When it came time to have the grown hogs butch-ered, we looked forward to getting a freezer full of hams, pork chops, roasts, ribs, and bacon to eat for many months into the future. So, it wasn't any traumatic thing for us to call the butcher shop and arrange for a man to come out, slaughter the animals, and take them back to the shop for processing. Just before he was scheduled to arrive, Kathy went out to the pen and thanked the hogs for the meat they would provide us. She did this in keep-ing with a tradition she had read about in which Native

Americans put grass in the mouths of the animals they killed to express their gratefulness for the sustenance the creature provided.

After our experience the first year, we were always happy to call the butcher and have him come to our place, instead of us hauling the pigs to him. That's what we tried to do the first time. I borrowed a small livestock trailer from Fred and backed it up to the pen. This would be easy, I thought, and enlisted Kathy's help in luring the hogs up a ramp and into the trailer, using plums to entice them. A relative of our neighbor, Elaine, had a plum orchard, and she invited us to come and pick all we wanted. A few days before we tried to load the pigs, we tossed a few plums their way, and they loved them. So, I laid down a trail of plums on the ground, and the pigs snatched them up quickly, but wouldn't step up on the ramp. After a frustrating few minutes, I got behind one of the 230-pound pigs and tried to push him along. No luck with that, either. The hog stiffened his legs, squealed loudly, and wouldn't budge. We tried everything we could to get one or the other into the trailer, but nothing worked. I didn't know what else to do, so I drove over to Fred's place and told him our predicament. Fred, who had raised pigs for many years in the past, said he would come over and stopped to get a rope out of his garage as he walked to his pickup. When we got back to our place, Fred stepped in the pen, got beside one of the hogs, and tied the rope around its neck, then looped it under a front leg and up the side of its shoulder. He pulled up on the rope, and the pig moved forward. Fred continued this process right up the ramp until the hog was in the trailer, and he repeated it with the other pig. Profusely thanking Fred for his help and sheepish over our greenhorn ways, Kathy and I got in the truck and took our hogs to the butcher shop. It was the only time we tried to haul pigs. Having the butcher come out proved to be a much better choice. Besides, Kathy said, plums should be put into jam, not into pigs.

If we became attached to our pigs, it was because there were only two of them in the pen, not dozens, and they had personalities. They would jump up on the fencing to get near us and see what goodies we might have for them. My goal was to keep them happy because happy pigs put on pounds faster than unhappy ones. We would get a pair of little 20-pound pigs from a farm in the area in early May and keep them through summer until they weighed 230-240 pounds, a good slaughter weight. They gave us a lot of laughs, and we enjoyed their antics, watching them race around the pen or play "soccer" with a round rock they dug up. When my niece and her children visited us one summer, her 5-year-old boy, Anthony, went over to see the pigs. Later, his mother placed a call to her husband and asked Anthony if he would like to say hello. Anthony excitedly told his dad that we had pigs, and that when one of them shoved its snout through the fence, he put his finger "in the hole where the boogers are!"

I always set up the pig shelter and pen on new ground each year to avoid spreading disease from one pair of pigs to the next. Keeping clean straw in the shelter also is a must, both for warmth in the early spring and for keeping the pigs clean. A muddy pig will go into the shelter at night, sleep on a bed of straw, and come out in the morning without a trace of the mud. I also made sure our pigs had clean water at all times, using a bucket with a stainless steel nipple that they learned to suck on. We fed our pigs a ration we bought at the feed store, but supplemented that with food scraps from our kitchen and whatever garden cuttings were available. They loved corn leaves and husks, rutabaga leaves, squash and zucchini, as well as wild pea vines cut from the meadows and hazel nuts. Kathy fed the pigs some excess tomatoes one year, and when we used the pig pen ground the next year for garden space, volunteer tomatoes appeared. Pigs need a mud hole to wallow in when it gets hot, so if it were necessary, I filled up a hole with water using a garden hose. Shade also is important, and if there weren't a tree nearby that shaded the pen, I would put up a tarp to create shade.

One pig provided us with enough pork for the year, but raising just one is not a good idea because pigs are social animals and need company. So we always raised two at a time. Relatives split the cost of butchering one of the pigs, and we butchered one for ourselves. They also shared the other costs.

While we had pigs from the start, we waited until the spring of 1999 to order our first batch of baby chicks. After reading a few good articles about chickens, I jumped in eagerly, setting up a box in the shop with heat lamps hanging above, ready for the chicks. Everything went smoothly during the eight weeks I had them in the shop, but I didn't realize how much dust fast-growing chicks kick up. By the time I put the chicks in the newly-built coop and fenced run, everything in the shop was completely coated with a layer of fine dust.

It took Kathy and me two hours to clean the place. In April of the next year, when I bought some more chicks to add to the flock, I reared them in the shop again. But, this time I put them in my trusty Apache trailer, not only covering the top with chicken wire so they couldn't get out, but also keeping a tarp over much of it to contain some of the dust. When they were old enough, and it had warmed up, I rolled out the trailer and backed it into the empty stall in my wood shed. I added on a small run so the chicks could go outside and onto the grass, and kept them there until they were big enough to be introduced to the other hens in the coop.

By then, we were getting a good supply of eggs from the first group of hens, and when the second group started laying that fall, we had sufficient eggs to start selling them to friends and people in the community. We raised dual-purpose chickens, meaning they are suitable for both eggs and meat. We kept the hens and butchered the roosters that were among the "straight run" chicks we ordered. Straight run means both male and female chickens will be included in the order, rather than just one particular sex. The breeds we chose were White Rock, Barred Rock, Buff Orpington, and Rhode Island Red, all which produce brown eggs. It was a pleasure to collect the eggs in our basket each day and know that they not only taste better than store-bought eggs, but also look better because of their dark yellow yolks.

I would have liked to let the hens roam freely in our yard, but with so many critters about, it just wasn't possible. Even with the chicken fencing, a fox found a hole in the run one summer and killed several hens. To compensate for the fact that they couldn't run freely, I did my best to keep them supplied with fresh grass, clover, dandelion leaves, pea vine, and garden waste, as well as a plentiful supply of clean water. When they heard me in the yard, the hens would race out of the coop's little door into the run and press up against the wire, waiting to see what I had to give them.

A friend of mine built a "chicken tractor" to keep his hens. A chicken tractor includes a small henhouse and run and has wheels and handles on it for easy transfer. It can be moved to new ground every few days so that the chickens have fresh grass and ground to dig in. Kathy and I thought of building one, but our problem is simple – we don't have enough level ground for a chicken tractor to work. Hills, rocks, and overgrown gopher mounds make much of the terrain in the meadows bumpy and unsuitable for a contraption like that.

One August day, my friend, Curt, and I caught five of my hens and put them in a dog carrier in the back of my pickup. Our mission was to deliver them to his son, who lived with his wife in Minneapolis. Apparently, it is permissible to have hens in your back yard there, but not roosters. The young couple wanted to have a few hens for eggs, and I had more hens than I needed, so I offered them some of mine. The couple made a henhouse in their back-yard shed and built a run out-side. After making the delivery, we drove to the Mall of America to have lunch with my daughter, who at the time managed the cosmetics department at Blooming-dale's. Curt had wondered what his attire should be for delivering chickens one moment and standing among gleaming department-store cosmetic counters the next. I could never give him a good answer, but at least we thought to remove our feed store caps when we went to lunch with my daughter in the mall that day.

Kathy and I didn't butcher chickens every year, but when we did, it was a team effort. I caught the birds, severed their heads with an ax, and then held them with their necks down in a bucket to bleed them. Kathy then dipped the chickens in hot water and plucked off their feathers. Next, I gutted the birds, removed their feet and turned them over to Kathy, who removed any remaining feathers and cut them up for freezing. We usually butchered 15-20 chickens at a time. Buddy and Tara would watch us intently from a short distance. After we were done butchering, I had to sneak away, when the dogs were occupied with something else, to bury the chicken entrails in the woods. Each time I dug as deep a hole as I could, but rocks and roots made it a difficult job. Later, I would discover that the entrails had been dug up. I still suspect the dogs, but can't be sure, and they would never tell, even if they could.

Berries make fine fare when picked fresh in the summer, but I also appreciate it when Kathy brings out a bag of blueberries, raspberries, strawberries, or cranberries in the middle of the winter. She works hard picking berries and preparing them for freezing. We planted six dwarf blueberry bushes and had to amend the soil because it wasn't acidic enough for blueberries to grow. But with sphagnum moss and rotted pine sawdust from a neighbor, we managed to change the soil sufficiently over time to allow the blueberries to flourish. We also raise our own raspberries, but go to a "u-pick" farm for our strawberries. And we always check to see whether there is a cranberry crop in the nearby bog. We have a good rhubarb patch and freeze a good supply for making pies and sauce during the winter. The asparagus patch only produces enough for fresh eating during the summer, so we don't freeze it.

The Centennial and Chestnut crabapple trees we have produce outstanding fruit that makes wonderful applesauce. Kathy adds a little cinnamon in her recipe when canning it in jars. When I planted our apple orchard, I tried to select early, mid-season and late-producing varieties that, hopefully, will make good apple cider when blended, as well as give us a supply of apples for fresh eating and pies. Our orchard consists of the following varieties:

Apple Trees

Hazen – Early

State Fair – Early

Wealthy – Early to Mid-Season

Sweet Sixteen (2) – Midseason

Haralson – Late

Plum Trees

Pipestone

Toka (pollinator)

Both the Sweet Sixteen and Haralson apples are good keepers, so these trees should yield plenty of apples to keep for at least part of the winter. Our plans are to purchase an apple cider press so that we can make our own apple cider once the trees bear fully. When I get up in the morning, after making a fire and starting the coffee, I drink a six- or eight-ounce glass of apple juice. I make no claims, but I think it helps keep down my cholesterol level. Our local food co-op keeps me supplied with an organic apple juice now, and I buy the juice by the case in gallon jugs. But I am hoping to augment that supply with my own juice in the future. The juice costs about $35 a case now, and that may seem like a lot, but when you think of it as medicine, the cost is minimal.

We work in three different garden spaces, each of them approximately 25x50 feet in size. Since there are only two of us, we don't need a lot of garden space, and we don't have any desire to grow more than we really need or can give away to our friends. Besides, neither one of us wants to take on more work than necessary. We add organic manure and compost to the soil each spring, along with some wood ashes every few years, and we don't use chemical fertilizers or pesticides. Our gardening philosophy is simple: Good soil produces good, strong plants, and good, strong plants mean less disease.

We do lose some plants to disease and to wildlife, but, by and large, enough other plants survive. Kathy weeds the garden religiously, and we sort of follow a guideline that I read about somewhere that says to weed every 10 days. If you do, the weeds don't have a chance to mature and rob the garden of its moisture. We don't use mulch to cut down on weeds because we think it requires more work to gather it and put it down than it does to weed on a regular basis. Mulching would help reduce moisture loss, and with dry seasons seeming to occur more frequently of late, we may have to rethink our position.

Our principal crops are radishes, lettuce, spinach, broccoli, green beans, squash, zucchini, tomatoes, peppers, carrots, cucumbers, rutabagas, potatoes, beets, and onions. Pumpkins and gourds also are favorites for fall decorating and to give to friends. We grow what we prefer to eat and try to discipline ourselves when we sit down to order seeds on a cold winter day, while thoughts of gardening dance in our head. Yes, growing Brussels sprouts might be fun, but I don't care for them, so why bother? Actually, I don't know of a vegetable Kathy doesn't like, so the decisions on what seeds to order and crops to grow have to do with my selfish tastes more than anything else, I suppose. But she graciously

15

Homestead Days, Buttoning Up

On November 10, 1998, a snowstorm roared through northern Minnesota, dumping 10 inches of snow and knocking down trees and power lines in a wide area. We lost our electricity at 1 p.m. that day and didn't get it back until four days later. Many trees toppled onto township roads, and Fred asked me if I would help our friend, John, clean up some of the worst-hit roads. Both Fred and John served on the township board at the time. The storm blew down more than 40 trees – mostly jack pines – on one road alone, and that is where we started. Firing up our chainsaws, we cut through large and small trees, throwing and pushing them to the side of the road as best we could, just to clear enough room for cars to pass. Later, we drove on other roads, looking for downed trees and cleaning up messes.

Two months before the big storm, I purchased a

generator and hired an electrician to install a box in our house so that I could switch to generator power when a power outage occurred. The electrician installed an outside receptacle, allowing me to send power from the generator into the house, and he wired the electrical box so that I would be able to keep the well, basement sump pump, and freezer operating. He also installed an outlet so that I could run power cords upstairs to a hotplate, toaster, coffee pot, and a few lights. So when the snow-storm hit, and our power went out, we managed quite well. Since we heat with wood, the house stayed warm, and we also could use the masonry heater's bake oven to cook a roast or bake a pie. Our neighbors were without power as well, but they didn't have a generator. Because we could operate our well pump, we supplied them with water for their horses.

Buying a generator was not high on our list of priorities, but for some reason we went ahead with the expenditures – $900 for the generator and $600 for the electrical box and wiring. Now, we see that we made a good decision to prepare for emergencies like the snow-storm. Every month or so, I start the generator and let it run for 10 minutes. By keeping it well maintained and running it on a regular basis, I can be sure the generator will start in an emergency. Putting gasoline stabilizer in the tank to make sure the gas stays fresh also helps. A generator sits most of the time, so taking these simple steps makes sense.

I enjoyed working with John when we cut up the trees on the roads following the big snowstorm. The next summer, we drove over all township roads, cleaning away brush and fallen trees in the ditches, as well as picking up trash. A few years later, we cut firewood together on county land. A logging crew was cutting oak, birch, and poplar on a large tract that butted up against my property. One day, I drove back on a logging road to see the head logger and asked him whether I could cut up any leftover fallen trees once his crew was finished logging. I mentioned that I would be able to have access to the tract's northern edge using my trails. The man said I could cut up anything that was left, and then to my surprise, he told me he would have one of his men clear a trail through the tract, connecting with my trail on the north end. That meant John and I could take my tractor and trailer and drive from one end of the tract to the other, cutting firewood wherever we found it. And cut we did. We hauled out many loads of firewood that fall and made stacks that we came back for the next year. The loggers left one pile of big logs, which we cut up and hauled away. We could only surmise that there weren't enough logs in the pile to justify sending back another truck, so they just left it for us. Later, some other friends came out with me, and we cut up several piles of big oak limbs.

Cutting firewood, whether alone or with friends, is a pleasant occupation. I think some people make it work by pushing too hard for too long a time. Most days, I like to cut a trailer load in the morning and maybe go back for another in the afternoon. If I get tired after the morning's work, that will be it for the day. Being outdoors, smelling the wood being cut, throwing the pieces into the trailer, and breathing in the clean, cool air – all this makes for a good day. John once brought along a few apples from his orchard, and he handed one to me when we took a break. Tara and Buddy, who had been running around at first, but now were resting in the sunshine, waited for us to toss the apple cores to them.

Safety is a primary concern in the woods, and I read both articles and books about using chainsaws and cutting down trees. But bad things can happen, even if you take precautions. Once, Kathy and I went into the woods to cut down a large dead standing oak tree. The

contractor took down many trees and piled up the logs. The owners didn't heat with wood and gave the logs to me if I would cut them up and haul them out. Kathy and I made numerous trips, loading up the Apache with oak, birch, maple, and poplar that we split and stacked in the wood shed. I always make sure to haul away all the leftover branches and debris and rake the area so it looks good when I leave. Friends call me when they have a tree that has fallen or needs to be removed, and ask me if I want the firewood. I usually say yes, unless it involves taking down a tree that is too close to a building or poses some risk. Those, I leave to professionals. Finally, if loggers are cutting in the immediate area, I will buy a permit from the county to cut firewood in the tract once the loggers have left. Nearly always, there is a large amount of firewood lying on the ground, waiting for someone like myself to cut it up and haul it away. One April, Kathy and I made early morning trips with my tractor and trailer to a nearby tract that had been cut over. The ground was still frozen in the early hour, so I could drive the tractor over the debris on the ground without any trouble, and we hauled away a load each morning all during Easter week. We were back in the yard by nine o'clock, and the firewood was split and stacked by 11.

Splitting wood has its pleasures, whether splitting by hand or using a machine. Until I bought a gasoline-engine powered wood splitter in 2005, I used a maul to split all my firewood. Sometimes the pile of cut-up logs in front of the wood shed seemed daunting, but I would take the first piece, put it on the stump and split it, keeping at it for an hour or so before taking a break. Then, I would repeat the process another one or two times during the day, until Kathy came home to help me stack the split wood in the shed. The next day, if the weather permitted, I would start the process all over again.

I have learned to keep my eye sharply focused on the exact spot where I want the splitting maul's sharp edge to meet the wood. By doing so, I usually hit the mark and complete a successful split. The eye, brain, and body work in unison. If I fail to concentrate and let my mind wander, I likely will miss the mark and end up hitting the log on the side, which sends it flying. Splitting wood, I have come to learn, teaches me to pay attention to what's in front of me and to focus on the goal I hope to achieve.

Another homestead job that I have come to appreciate is making maple syrup. Syrup making is probably in my blood because my mother's grandparents operated a maple-syrup farm in Quebec. With no sugar maple trees on our land, I was lucky to have the chance to help a group of men who collect sap each spring near a large recreational lake in our area. I took a couple of the fellows back to the logged area where John and I had been cutting firewood, and they cut some for themselves. When they were leaving, one of them gave me a quart of maple syrup he had made. He asked me whether I would like to join the maple syrup group the next spring. I jumped at the chance. The men boil down the maple tree sap they collect to a certain point and then distribute it among themselves in plastic gallon jugs. Each worker takes home his share and boils it down further. Learning about the boiling-down process from the Internet, I set up a hot plate on our picnic table and sheltered it from the cool mid-April wind. There I boiled the sap, one gallon at a time, down to about a quart of syrup. The process takes a while, so patience is necessary. When I was finished, Kathy poured the hot syrup into jars and then put on canning lids.

When I was a boy and saw my mother preparing pancake batter, I always asked her, "Are they going to be big ones or little ones?" When she answered, "Big ones," I was happy because the "big ones" were French crepes – plate-size, thin pancakes made with eggs, flour, and milk. The "little ones" were the kind you get from a box of Aunt Jemima pancake mix. When we moved to Hiram Hill, I was determined to get my mother's French pancake recipe from my sister, Shirley, who makes them for her family. Now, I make crepes for myself quite often, pouring on some maple syrup, rolling them up, and enjoying the wonderful taste. Sometimes I choose to eat them with our homemade chokecherry syrup, another great-tasting treat. Kathy isn't as fond of French pancakes as I am, but the dogs are. When they get the scent of the pancakes in the frying pan, they wait at the door until I can share some with them.

Shirley also makes her own bread using my mother's recipe. But when I asked her for the recipe, she had to think for a while because she didn't follow one. Everything was in her head. She wrote down the recipe for me, and now I make all our bread and buns. Kathy and I amended the recipe to include more whole-wheat flour and ground-up flax seed, but otherwise it is the same. I make five loaves at a time, unless we use some of the dough for buns. At other times, I make cinnamon rolls, especially if we're going to have company. When my mother made bread, I always saw her make the Sign of the Cross when she mixed in the yeast. She told me that she signed herself to assure that the bread would rise. If she didn't make the Sign of the Cross, she was certain the batch of bread would fail. So, I follow her practice today. I also get pleasure out of knowing that the bread board I use to knead the dough is the same one she used on our farm in northwestern Minnesota.

Using something from the past to create something new appeals to both Kathy and me. She cut up my old plaid flannel shirts – those I wore while we built our place – to make two quilted sampler wall hangings depicting scenes from Hiram Hill. After sewing on loops at the top of the hangings, she cut tree branches and slipped them through the openings to use as hangers. Kathy also made a sampler quilt for our bed with fabric from my old shirts and her old plaid skirts and jumpers.

During the winter of 2002-2003, we lacked snow cover in our area and experienced many very cold days. The frost penetrated down more than 10 feet in some areas, and frozen septic systems became a common problem. People lost use of their septic systems for months, and septic tank service workers were working long hours trying to thaw pipes. Some lake cabin septic systems didn't thaw out until late April and even into May. We were fortunate that ours did not freeze, even though that year I had not put any straw or leaves over the pipe leading from the house to the septic tank. Straw and leaves serve as insulation and prevent the frost from penetrating deeply into the ground. Normally, with a good snow cover, septic systems don't freeze, especially when they are in use every day. But if people go on vacation or use their place as a cabin getaway, their septic systems sit idle for periods of time. In such situations, frost builds up in pipes, and when owners return and flush waste down into the system, it becomes trapped in the frost and eventually plugs the pipes, then freezes. The lesson of 2002-2003 taught me not to take any chances, so raking up leaves to put over our septic pipes and tank now is a mandatory undertaking in my annual pre-winter "buttoning up" of Hiram Hill.

I like the term, "buttoning up," and I like the process it entails. Being near the end of another year, another cycle of seasons, it is a time to take stock, clean up, dispose of, put away, and protect. It is a time to look back, as well as a time to look ahead; a time to assess the progress you've made and prepare for the progress you hope to make in the coming year. It is a deliberate time, a step-by-step course of action, not to be hurried, compromised, or curtailed. No one should be too busy to button up properly for winter. The act of buttoning up is a statement of gratitude for what has been entrusted to you. It is an encouragement to loved ones, who take comfort in seeing that care, order, and attention to detail still count in a hectic and confused world. If everyone took time to "button up" – if everyone took care of the matters entrusted to them – the world would be a better place. The matter of buttoning up, then, is no small matter, but counts meaningfully in the larger order of things.

Buttoning up begins in the middle of October, when the lawn mowers are serviced and put away until spring. I change the engine oil, clean the air filter and spark plug, sharpen the cutting blades, clean the underside of the deck, and wipe away all dirt and grease. A little stabilizer in the tank keeps the gas fresh through the winter. When the mower is put away, the snow blower is brought out. Since it was serviced last spring, it is ready to do its work. Then it's time to hook the Apache on the tractor and go about the yard, picking up benches, lawn chairs, and the picnic table to store in the barn. By then, most of the garden has been cleaned up, except for the decorative corn shock. That goes to the burn pile. The garden won't be tilled, and the soil, with its billions of microorganisms at work, will sit undisturbed until spring. Kathy cleans up the flower beds, and I cut down the peonies and lay the stalks over the roots for insulation. There are leaves to rake, both for the compost pile and to cover the septic system, and there are always broken branches to pick up. If the pile of firewood has been split and stacked, I rake up the remaining pieces of bark and wood chips and throw them into the woods. Ferris drives over with a couple of his John Deere mowers to store in my barn, so I rearrange things there to prepare for his arrival. Just picking up the hoses used to irrigate the gardens with pond water takes a half hour or so, and I also empty the water out of the pump and put it in the barn. Dumping the water out of the rain barrel, I flip it over to keep out snow. A check of the firewood rack sitting alongside the shop shows that more dry wood should be added so there is plenty to burn over winter. I trim some tree branches, hauling them to the burn pile, where a mighty fire will roar once snow covers the ground. And, I walk to each bluebird box, taking out the abandoned nests of blue-

COMING FULL CIRCLE

In the middle of September, 1960, I boarded a train in a tiny town near our farm and rode it to Minneapolis, where I got on a Jefferson Lines bus to Kansas City. I was 18 and on my way to Columbia, Missouri, to start my freshman year at the University of Missouri. The express bus breezed through southern Minnesota and northern Iowa, stopping only in Mason City, before continuing on to Des Moines. There, a young man my age got on the bus and sat down next to me. As the bus pulled out of the station, I asked him where he was headed. "Fort Hays State College in Hays, Kansas," was his answer. Fort Hays State College? I had never heard of it before. The thought that one of its graduates would someday profoundly change my life never crossed my mind. He told me Hays was located in the western part of the state, and that he had never been there. My story was the same. I had never been to Columbia. In fact, I had never been far from home. When we got to the station in Kansas City, he transferred to a bus going to Hays, about 270 miles west. I went east 125 miles to Columbia.

There we were, two young men going off on separate paths, venturing to new places, and chasing different dreams. I would go to Mizzou to earn a journalism degree, start a career, and marry. I don't know what happened to him. But I do know that the name of that Kansas college, and the conversation I had with that young man, echoed in my mind many years later, when, on our first date, Kathy told me she was a graduate of Fort Hays State College – now called Fort Hays State University.

◊ ◊ ◊

Although the November sun hangs low in the sky, there still is enough time to take a walk before it gets dark. Tara bounds out of the garage when I open the front door. "Let's go for a run, Tara." She runs up to me, as she always does, looking for affirmation before she takes off across the lawn and down the trail leading to the barn. I follow her, but stop on the trail to take a good look at the barn. The red stain is really holding up

around, I head back to the main trail, rejoining it in the meadow and following it up the hill to the homestead. Tara and I walk past the Trinity trees, and I stop to look at the rocks marking the graves of Kirby, Buddy, and Amanda's cat, Murphy. The 40 or so red pines I planted just down the slope are flourishing, and now, with the leaves off the other trees, I can see them clearly. They are becoming a favorite haunt of deer. Tara and I cut across the tall grass to another short trail that leads us to Beaver Point. I love to stand on that little hill and look back to the south and east, across the wetland and over to the big pond and the fields beyond. The shadows are getting longer now. I pick up my pace and walk through the woods to our gravel driveway. There, I think about how much work it was to clear the 400 feet of woods, and how the curves in the road add mystery to the drive up. When I reach the top of the driveway, I notice that I haven't removed the old nest of Mrs. Phoebe, who comes each year to our storage shed. I built a little platform for her nest just under the eave. It's a safe place for her to lay eggs and raise her young, and we enjoy her presence each summer. By now, Tara is back in the garage in her tent. I walk toward the house, then stop and turn to look back at the shop, wood shed, chicken coop, and the high, leafless tree line in back. The sun has set now, and it is getting dark. I turn back toward the house, and the warm yellow light of the kitchen shines through, inviting me in. I can see Kathy standing at the sink. I step into the house and close the door. The radiant heat from the masonry heater warms my face, and I can smell supper on the stove. We'll sit down at the table in a few minutes, but now the easy chair beckons me, and I settle into its arms. Looking up, I see Kathy's painting hanging above the sofa. It's been a long walk, but I'm home again.

Homestead Recipes

My mother passed down these recipes to my sisters, who in turn gave them to me. I altered the bread recipe to include whole wheat flour and ground flax seed, as well as less salt, but otherwise they remain as passed down.

White/Whole Wheat Bread

3 lbs. whole wheat flour

3 lbs. white unbleached flour

1 1/2 cups ground flax seed

3/4 cup margarine or butter

1 tablespoon salt

1/3 cup sugar

2 quarts water

7 teaspoons dry yeast

Fill a two-quart sauce pan with approximately one

quart of water. Place margarine, sugar, and salt in the water. Heat until margarine is dissolved. Add a quart of cold water to the top of the pan. Allow the mixture to cool down, but still remain warm.

Dissolve yeast in 2/3 cup of warm water. Allow to stand until yeast is dissolved.

Mix together flour and ground flax seed in large bowl. Make a well in the center of the mixed flour. When the margarine/sugar/salt mixture has cooled down, but still remains warm, pour it into the flour well and add the dissolved yeast. Mix together until all the flour is worked in, adding a little flour as needed if the dough is sticky. Transfer the dough onto a floured board and knead it with hands for five or more minutes. Add flour as needed until dough is no longer sticky. Put the dough in a large bowl, brush with melted margarine, and cover with a dish towel. Place in a warm area.

After it has risen to one inch or so over the top of the bowl, remove the dough and knead again lightly on the bread board so any gas bubbles are released. Then, cut the dough and form into loaves or buns (25-28 ounce portions for loaves and 2 1/2 ounce portions for buns). Place in greased baking pans. Bake loaves 40 minutes at 380 degrees. Bake buns 25 minutes. Dough also may be used to make cinnamon rolls, if desired. Bake rolls same as buns. When baking is done, place the bread on racks to cool. Makes five loaves or approximately five dozen buns.

French-Canadian Pancakes (Crepes)

1 1/2 cups flour

1/8 teaspoon salt

1 1/2 cups milk

3 eggs

Beat ingredients with a whisk until the batter is smooth. Add enough milk so that the batter is fairly thin. Put a small amount of shortening in a 10-inch fry pan and heat. Pour in 1/4 cup of batter and rotate the fry pan until the batter is spread as evenly and thinly as possible. Cook until the underside is golden brown, then flip the pancake over using a table knife and fork, or spatula and fork. Makes 10 pancakes.

Chokecherry Syrup

1/2 cup white corn syrup

2 cups chokecherry juice

3 cups sugar

Put the chokecherries into a sauce pan. Add water to cover. Boil until the berries break down. Press and drain the juice through cheesecloth.

Mix the juice, syrup, and sugar. Bring to boil. Reduce heat and simmer for 15 minutes. Pour into pint jars. Seal with canning lids. Makes two pints. Excellent topping for pancakes.

Crème au Sucre

2 cups brown sugar

2 cups heavy cream

2/3 cup shelled hazel nuts or unsalted peanuts

Heat the cream and sugar in a saucepan just until the sugar is dissolved. Remove from heat. Cool. Add nuts at the time you serve it. Crème au sucre is eaten as a sauce or can be used as topping for ice cream. It was a candy treat served in French Canadian homes on holidays.

Printed in the United States
131506LV00001B/1/P